Falling into the Mystery...

Zahir Khan

To my mother and father and You

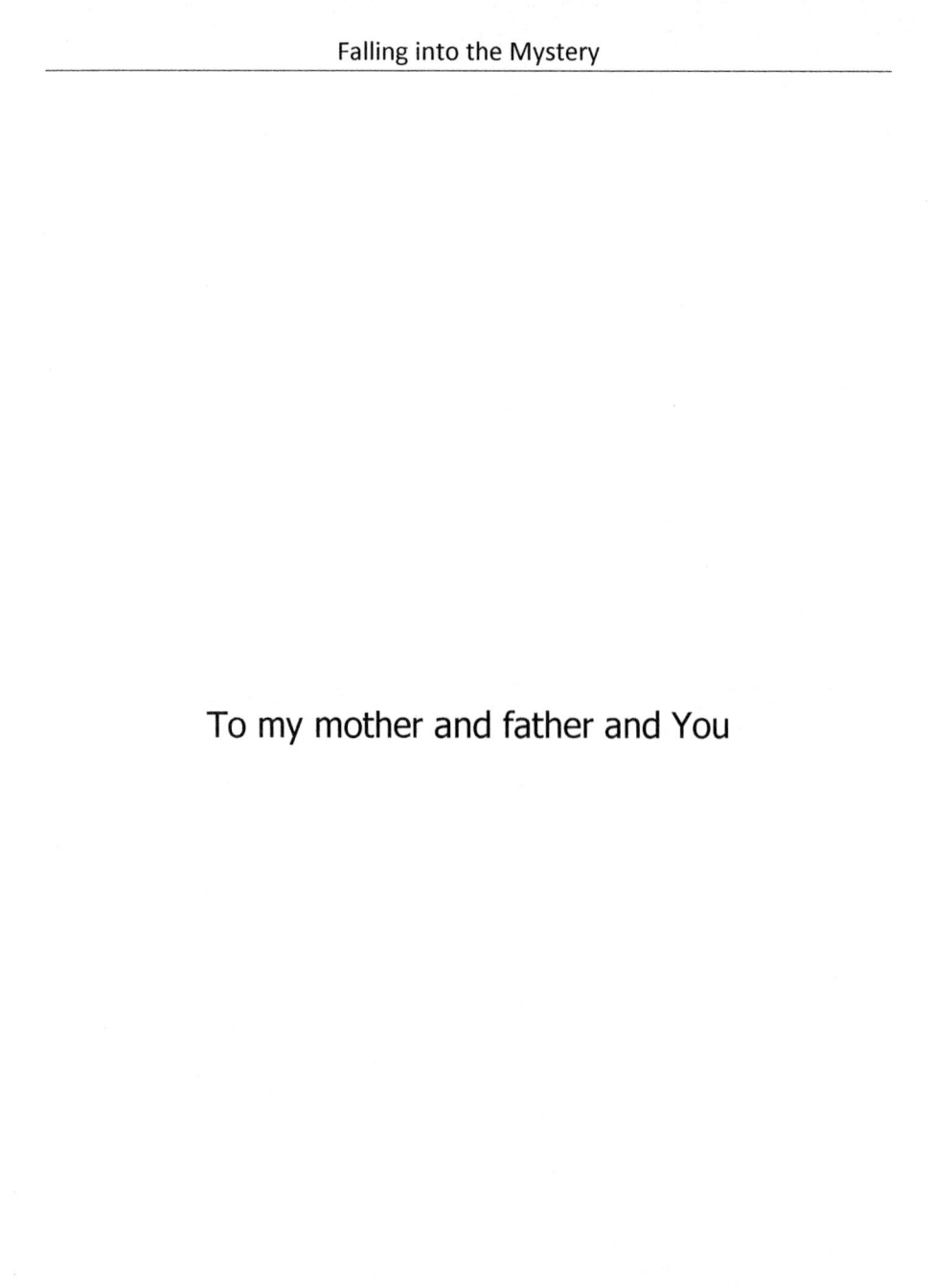

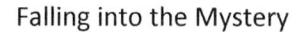

I'm falling into the mystery and I'm losing myself and yet even as I lose myself I find myself. What I really am and what I am capable of. It is a mass of emotions, feelings, thoughts and ideas, and yet finally after all these years it now all makes sense.

Table of Contents

In the beginning... 5

The teacher of the ages... 8

The old man's coat... 25

It's all an illusion... 33

In the Garden again... 66

The old ways... 82

The Sufi and the Faqir... 91

I need to be recognized today... 116

Rumi... 129

Dervish... 134

Death... 137

What happened next... 142

Did you think I'd forgotten... 169

Glossary... 171

In the beginning...

Thoreau stated

"Many men lead lives of quiet desperation and go to the grave with the song still in them"

Society rushes forward and yet as people we move backwards. Every ego impulse is satiated and yet as people we are no closer to being happier. We have a myriad of ways to communicate but despite or maybe because of social media, emails and 24 hour access to the world, we still can't talk and form real human connections. Divorces, depression and suicides are at record highs, unjust wars are fought in our names, people are radicalised and society lurches from one disaster to the next. There is always the desire to be bigger, better, faster and stronger, always another gadget to buy, another experience to be had and as we spin faster and faster on the merry go round that is our life, our tenuous grip loosening with each whirl, we hope maybe just maybe the next experience may set us free. Free from the maddening pace of life and we will be able to sit as we did when we were children. Sit, stare and finally be free.

For a while I thought of such things and wondered if there was a way to break free of an existence with no meaning. In that sense I was no different from many others but at the time I felt I was the only one going through such feelings and thoughts. The nagging feeling that things could be better but not knowing how to go about making my life better.

After many years of questioning myself, of failed attempts to improve my life the idea of becoming free and enlightened gathered momentum.

In that moment the idea of "Freedom" appeared to be the cure to all of life's failings, so I started seeking. I read across traditions, religions, about enlightened personalities all offering me hope of betterment. The yearning however to both physically and mentally experience their enlightenment continued to haunt me.

It was at this turbulent juncture that I decided to leave my hometown and relocate into hidden isolation. I was in my early thirties carrying foreboding feelings of death.

I decided to move to Scotland, Glasgow to be specific to ascertain whether shrouding in isolated solitude would answer my questions and unlock my freedom.

Hence this story is about my journey to finding ultimate freedom. I do not intend to write an autobiography, even though at times it may read as an autobiography, I merely intend to encapsulate the idea of freedom into the reality of actually realising freedom.

The book may seem disjointed at times but rest assured it will all make perfect sense in the end. Whilst the thoughts and ideas may not follow a linear form, it is in fact a complete work.

It has been several years since I ceased searching and instead started talking with people about my experiences and attempting to help others resolve their spiritual seeking. This then is an attempt to convey my thinking on the subject of self-realisation. Others have written on the subject of enlightenment, awakening and freedom, but this is my contribution to the subject. At this point in my life I am compelled to relay my experiences, my answers. I have learned that in this life change is the only constant and no doubt my thinking will change in the future. This then is an attempt to take a snapshot in time.

The teacher of the ages...

The idea of enlightenment is a beguiling one. Imagine it if you will. Enlightenment is the only cure you will ever need for all your troubles. Bliss on tap and a knowing which will ensure that your life never knows pain or suffering. Perfect health, wealth, relationships and wisdom all packaged in the intoxicating haze of pure ecstasy! It is an enticing idea and this idea is sold to millions of new seekers every year and as the hordes of ever smiling seekers and gurus grow exponentially year in year out, all looking for the holy grail of enlightenment. Why would you not then start to believe that this is the answer you have been looking for? I know I certainly was smitten by the idea.

I was twenty three having lost my father to cancer and with several other events all happening simultaneously I deteriorated from being a confident young man with life planned out to an insecure young man fearing every aspect of life. Golden boy went from hero to zero in three easy steps over six months. It was then that the solution to all of my troubles entered my life. Enlightenment came along and as I swallowed the bait everything went all hazy while I lay back ready to enjoy the ride, I knew life was never going to be the same. I was now a seeker.

I wasn't just a seeker though; I was now an aspiring Sufi. Having been invited to a Sufi festival by a friend, I met a man claiming to be a Sufi master. He was not just any old Sufi master but the master of the current age. In my ignorance of all things spiritual I accepted everything on offer and took the "bayat" (pledge of allegiance) to the man who would become my teacher. He ticked all the boxes, a wizened old man with long white hair, long beard and a knowing look. That confident assured depth of knowledge in his eyes enticed me to become his pupil. I sank further into accepting the love of his other students as I continued to search for someone to guide me out of the mess that my life had become.

The idea of becoming a Sufi and synchronising in equivalent enlightenment as the teacher was appealing and even though this maddening desire would encapsulate me years later, the seed had already been planted and I found myself becoming a student.

It was a Sunday morning and I had spent an entire night of whirling, listening to spiritual music known as qawalli and hearing constant compliments about the teacher's greatness. The benefits of being his student had been sold to me and this became the catalyst to me taking the plunge. I was instructed in the basic ideas of Sufism, shown how to perform certain meditations and away I went.

I recall that as I was sitting with the teacher he cryptically said to me and another student

"You will be teachers and in your lineage will be teachers"

The student with me burst into tears and bowed at the teacher's feet. I stayed silent not realising that I had just started a journey which would devour the next eight years of my life and fill my life with madness.

Those years taught me about the Sufi way and I read every book I could find on the Sufis and sat with the senior students of the school. To say I knew what I was doing would be a lie, frankly I was out of my depth and nothing I did was sufficient. I was not even aware whether I was making progress.

I started to distance myself from the teacher on his visits to the UK or if I found myself in his presence. I used every convenient excuse to retreat from him. I was in total awe and fear of him. Nothing he said made sense and I struggled to carry out any basic practices he relayed. I struggled to figure it all out and I found myself on a slippery slope and my despair and inability to make sense of what I was learning deepened.

Several years into this despair I received an invitation to travel to Pakistan to attend a Sufi festival. I was now wary of the teacher as by now my views and faith in the man I had chosen as my teacher had been severely shaken after hearing stories of financial impropriety and sexual abuse. A fellow student and dear friend offered to pay my fare to Pakistan, I would learn later he was coerced into it by senior students and with the constant phone calls from fellow students all extolling the spiritual benefits of the festival and how it would improve my life I once again took the plunge.

I arrived in Pakistan and immediately realised why I had been summoned. The younger son of the teacher whom I had only ever spoken to over the phone had organised my trip. Intellectually and spiritually this young man was a giant. His personal library held over two thousand books, covering every manner of text on the spiritual endeavour. I had myself been asked to find two rare volumes of Sufi thought for the library of this spiritual genius.

His genius was such that many who had tried to debate him came away defeated. It was generally acknowledged that with his brilliance, he was the person most likely to succeed the teacher. This was something I would hear time and time again in Sufi schools in Pakistan. Generally when the time came for the teacher to pass on, he would name a successor who was known as the "Gaadi Nashin". Nine times out of ten he would be chosen from within the teachers own family.

Although it could be argued that the son had spent most time with his father/teacher, I suspect it was more of an economic argument that won the day. The teacher would have spent a lifetime building up a movement, primarily this movement would be cash rich with students constantly donating and helping propagate the teachers work. It made sense to prevent the stream of income going into an outsider's hand to choose the successor from within the teacher's lineage.

The son was recruiting for his own inner circle and unknown to me I had been selected. I suppose I should have been flattered that the son of the teacher wanted to see me, but as my time progressed there I realised he had an ulterior negative motive.

I was asked about other students and the day to day affairs of the students in England and I quickly realised it was about installing me as some kind of organiser, promoter and spy of the school and its students in England. The teacher was suspicious that some of his senior students were engaged in financial improprieties and wanted information. After all they were taking money that was destined for him and he was not happy about this. The teacher was using his son to extract information from me.

I was western educated and born in England unlike the majority of other students, I was viewed as someone who would not try to play politics and provide straight answers. The abuse of power by the teacher and senior students was now spreading throughout the school. I listened to everything and nodded my assent where needed, knowing deep down that I wanted to be anywhere but here.

I danced, I whirled and whirled and whirled and as I whirled my confusion, my depression, my anger became stronger. I couldn't understand this path I was on. Why couldn't I figure it out? With each whirl I went faster and faster and sights, sounds and life became a blur, the only thing remaining was my confusion which seemed to rise and rise. Finally I could take no more and involuntarily let out a cry. I wanted out of this, out of life, out of everything, my despair knew no bounds and as I continued whirling I felt someone grab hold of me. My instinct was to push them away but I realised I had lost use of my arms and legs. A silence engulfed me and I was no longer there. Time ceased. I ceased. There was nothing.

I regained consciousness after how long I don't know and remember being held up, one of the senior students was massaging my heart and as I looked out another senior student asked me,

"Where are you brother?"

"I'm here" I replied.

I stared out across the assembled students, the qawwals. In the midst of this the teacher looked at me knowingly.

The next day there was an unknown peace inside me, peace that I had never experienced before. I had gone to bed shattered and now as I walked across the garden in the home of the teacher there was a silence in me. Silence and finally peace.

Students who met me kissed my hands. I neither stopped them nor encouraged them. I was just quiet. All that remained was this peaceful silence. I sat down to eat with some of the other students and as words formed to answer the questions put to me all I felt was profound peace.

The festival ended and after another week I returned to the United Kingdom. Something had changed although it still remains difficult to explain the exact nature of change. I found myself increasingly at peace within myself and with no real desire to meet any of my fellow students. I stopped attending gatherings, content instead to spend time alone. The students started narrating tales that I had been blessed with so much spiritual power that I was unable to handle it. It was their way of trying to understand why I had stopped answering calls or meeting them. No one seemed to understand how I could just end contact after all I had experienced in the two weeks that I spent in Pakistan. My teacher had been happy with me and his son and I had spent so much time together. Many spiritual treasures had been bestowed upon me and yet I had chosen to relinquish all contact.

Of that time all I can say is I no longer felt the desire to meet anyone or be like anyone. I was content, yes I knew I had not completed my journey but I was happy to just rest and take time out for myself. There had been nagging doubts but even they had subsided. I just felt different and yet that seemed just right at that time.

After a few months of being alone I was approached by some ex-students claiming that the teacher was in fact a charlatan. As story after story was narrated to me I remained untouched. I felt no anger no pain no regret of my time with this man. Deep down I always knew something was wrong and yet I was too weak too uncertain to do anything. I had hung around too long, desperate that the teacher would discredit my doubts and provide me with the answers I yearned for. In that sense his power had overtaken me just as I had surrendered my power to him.

In classical Sufism it is said that the student should totally capitulate to his teacher. In the hands of an authentic teacher that would make sense, but in the hands of a charlatan as I was, it becomes dangerous territory. This teacher had been my Rumi, my Ibn Arabi, and now it was over. As the stories continued and one ex-student appeared after another I knew I had to do something, not out of anger or hate but out of compassion for the students still there.

I arrived at the house of a fellow student who had also become a dear friend and brother. This man like me had spent many years with the teacher and later I would find out had donated in the region of twenty five thousand pounds to the teacher. Other senior students had also taken advantage of his good nature and he had lent them money too. Regardless of this he was at the time a staunch and loyal follower of the teacher. To say I was nervous would be an understatement.

He met me at the railway station and we went to his house, what happened next I will never forget. I calmly stated my case and relayed to him several stories of financial and sexual abuse experienced by other students. There was silence as he looked at me and I noticed the terrifying conflict he was experiencing. His eyes were confused, scared and angry. An entire rainbow of emotions was being played out in his eyes and finally after what seemed an eternity he spoke,

"Brother this man named my children".

He repeated,

"Brother this man named my children".

Like a mantra he repeated this statement as if saying this would make the very real pain he was feeling would go away. He repeated not to anyone in particular, it just had to be repeated. Occasionally he would lapse into silence and then the same thing

"Brother this man named my children".

I looked at him and offered to once again swear an oath if he was not convinced. He was silent and then looked at me and said,

"No, brother I trust you".

I could not believe what I had heard, could this be true? I was shocked and yet humbled that this man had trusted me. We had been close and he had been the brother who had paid my fare to Pakistan so I really wanted to save this man and his family as I loved him dearly. He was hurt but this hurt was nothing compared to what could have happened in his ignorance.

We spent the rest of the day together, him cancelling a ticket to Pakistan that he had booked to visit the teacher. He also accompanied me to see other students, some of whose reactions were less then favourable but throughout the entire day he stayed with me like a rock, risking personal harm to himself and his family.

He lived in the same town as many other students of the teacher and he received many menacing threats from fellow students, who were angered and declared him wrong. I had been fortunate to remove students in my hometown out of the school so I remained safe from the abuse my friend suffered. Yet he stood firm, even when the teacher declared across the entire school that I and the other brother who had been instrumental in helping students leave were apostates and outside the folds of Islam.

Indeed some of the senior students went further and declared that verses in the Holy Quran spoke of me and another ex-student as devils. It was a tough time but we were finally free of this man. I did in a momentary lapse speak to the teacher again and as he harangued me over the phone I realised that all this old man had was empty words. I quietly said goodbye and walked away. I was finally free of this charlatan.

Eight years however had lapsed and I was still no nearer to finding freedom.

Time rolled on and whilst those who had left the previous teacher joined other schools and found new teachers I slipped back into depression and my desperation to go free deepened. Allied to this I remembered students saying that those who did not have a teacher had the devil as a teacher. I therefore desperately searched for a new teacher but failed to find one.

With this dilemma at hand interesting questions submerged my mind. Did I really need a teacher? How would I know if he was authentic? Could I really surrender to another teacher absolutely given my previous experience?

Around this time I also came across self-help and was convinced I could go free myself. I therefore questioned whether it was right to hand over all my personal power to a teacher. Yes if the teacher was authentic, but as I stated earlier I was faced with the quandary of how I would recognise an authentic teacher.

If we look at the dynamics of the teacher and student relationship we find that it is one of mutual dependency despite the teacher holding a senior position. The student needs the teacher to guide his direction to attain liberation or transmit enlightenment to him.

On the other hand the teacher needs the student to verify him, after all if a teacher had no students, how would others know he was a teacher. The student also carries out other tasks like promoting the teacher and bringing other students to him, to help disseminate the teachings and build the school. As a senior student had said to me once, the students are the ones who build the school. Would certain teachers have been as well known had it not been for their disciples? Granted these men built huge followings but the same principle applies to any teacher with a large or small following. It is the students that illuminate the teacher's name. The teacher needs them if his teachings are to survive through time. Indeed one of the most successful teachers through time was Shams Tabriz, the teacher of Rumi. Rumi wrote of his love and all he had learnt from Shams thereby spreading the teaching of Shams and immortalising his story.

The intricate relationship between Rumi and Shams left me with the conclusion that a teacher's knowledge and guidance was indeed required yet I was unable to find one with the depth of truth that would help me enlighten.

My despair was compounded by the thought that on the Day of Judgement I would be one of those that would perish in the hellfire as I had no teacher to intercede on my behalf. Although these ideas of perishing in hell disintegrated over the years when I encountered more authentic teachings, at that time I was still subconsciously in thrall to the teacher. I had been indoctrinated that I required a teacher yet I knew I could no longer submit one hundred percent to a teacher.

It was around this time I started to read of people who had woken up or were spiritually awakened without following the traditional path of following a teacher. These people had somehow found God, and yet they had not been initiated into any school or in some cases even met their master or even a master. Here I found a glimmer of hope and an idea formed in my mind, maybe just maybe I could become enlightened. This idea of charting a course to my liberation was a revelation.

I also finally admitted that I wanted to be enlightened. What a relief it was to finally admit my dirty little secret. Prior to this when I had been with the teacher, all of us students would never have admitted that we were only there because we wanted to go free.

Instead statements of unworthiness of being nothing and receiving nothing abounded. There was in it all a false humility, the constant bowing and scraping in front of the teacher and to senior students. All really done to prove to others how humble we were and how we were fighting our ego. We were always in fear of making mistakes and nothing was ever good enough. Everything was criticised with the odd compliment thrown in to keep us coming back for more. We lived on tenterhooks feigning that we were happy but if we had really thought about it, we were all unhappy.

Taxi drivers, takeaway workers, the unemployed, the rejected and lower echelons of society all gathered together in a rag tag band believing they had been rejected by a society that failed to recognise who they truly were. We were broken but too scared to admit it. We railed against a society that had rejected us and yet in actual fact maybe we had rejected society first. We were failures, too scared to take responsibility for our lives and to go out and stake our claims to life. We had been brought together and our weaknesses manipulated.

As a group we felt we had been rejected not for being personally wrong, but because society was wrong. We as a group and as individuals were taught that we were right and it was society that failed to recognise our true worth. Indeed we were made to believe that the all mighty teacher had spiritually guided us without even being physically present and had eventually revealed himself to us to confirm that we were "God's chosen ones".

It was a heady mix and this in turn bred a spiritual arrogance in us. How could others know of the greatness of the teacher and of his teaching? How could those who did not have understanding understand us? Even as students began leaving when the truth was revealed the senior students created stories to cover the truth that the teacher was merely testing us and shedding students. Apparently he was creating situations to test our resolve and only the most committed would remain.

We were indoctrinated that whatever we heard or saw was not to be questioned and was just a test from the omnipotent master. As the "chosen ones" we were merely being tested through great trials and tribulations. I had been brainwashed to ignore what I knew was true that this man was a sexual predator and master manipulator. We were just ignorant pawns in his game and all semblances of intelligence and reality had been stripped from us. We were in a dire state.

Refocusing on my initial desire to end my suffering was like a jolt of electricity. I was back on track and armed with this knowing that really I wanted to be free of my pain and that others had achieved it without recourse to teachers or teachings. I was reinvigorated to pursue the goal. There was but one huge problem. How do I do this? Again despair set in and I found myself once more on the cold hard floor again. I found myself needing to begin again.

After a while it dawned on me that I should focus on reading the biographies of those who had achieved self-realisation and follow their approaches and teachings. In that sense it wasn't really a huge shift since I had substituted one teacher for a multitude of others. Around this period I researched meditation, psychology, different spiritual approaches and sadly concluded after extensive practical application of the techniques that nothing was going to work.

All the approaches in my mind were telling me something was wrong and it needed fixing, if only I could work through my issues. The proverbial peeling back of the layers of the onion, this felt like a long term approach and again I felt it would take too long and thus I was never going to be fixed or good enough to go free. In that sense it was just like the school I had left adding one more thing, that once all my issues were resolved at some point in the future I would receive the prize but only if I did the work.

I had changed direction from wanting to receive freedom from an omnipotent teacher to finding my own way to freedom, but again I had no guarantee that I would go free. How would I even know if I was free? Once again I was stuck.

The old man's coat...

Life carried on with this energy sapping state of affairs. I was sleepwalking through life and my depression and desperation with life was integrating deeper. All I did was to no avail and I just seemed to be on a downward spiral of negativity. This in turn impacted my relationships and my health. I steadily started putting on weight, retreating from life and not meeting friends. I argued with everyone and was generally angry and resentful of anyone whose life was working.

I was angry, the world had wronged me. Looking back on that time I see that I was just surviving. Externally I was in turmoil and internally I was falling apart. I tried everything to make my failing life work. I even married believing as did my family that I would snap out of it. Nine months later we were history and I was nowhere nearer to my goal, I now had a failed marriage alongside a failed suicide attempt. My resume of failure was filling out. I was adding even more pain and suffering to my life. I was cashing cheques with Karma that I really could not honour and the time bomb that was my life ticked away. It was only a matter of time before it blew and indeed it did but in the most unexpected of ways.

I had arranged to meet my sister at the shops to go shopping together. We entered a department store and I decided to try on a coat that I liked. As I put it on my sister turned to me and said,

"You can't buy that. It's like an old man's coat."

A simple remark, but something inside of me snapped and a terrifying thought entered that if remained here I would die. That remark summarised for me all my failures in life, yet this remark which brought me to my knees would also be the remark that would save me in the future.

It was on that Wednesday afternoon that I stood in the bus station queue to buy a ticket to Scotland. Ten minutes earlier I had decided to leave Coventry and not return until I achieved my goal of going free. My plan was simple I would go to the highlands in Scotland and meditate or just be still until I was free. If I did not go free I would just die on whichever hill, mountain or forest I was in. It was that simple. Death was preferable to this humiliation. I had told a friend I was just going to catch the overnight coach and arrive in Glasgow. That friend would then take me up to the highlands and I would stay there.

I switched off my phone and boarded the coach. Behind me, as if saying my goodbyes for me, the sun set on the concrete jungle that was my city darkening it out of my life. The coach moved off and again I was on course for my goal. Everything was a blur as we raced past cities and towns. I could not make out anything in the dark so fell asleep.

I awoke as the day was dawning and saw the spectacular countryside of Scotland. I was stiff from sleeping in a coach seat so took some time to fully awake and really appreciate the beauty I could now see. It was beautiful and unlike anything I had ever seen. I marvelled at this beauty and could not take my eyes off it. This place was truly beautiful and inside I smiled as I thought how amazing my life would be when I went free.

I arrived in Glasgow and after loading up on supplies of dried dates, a tent and sleeping bag, I headed with my friend to the highlands. She never expressed what her thoughts were but she was gracious enough to help me. As she left me I panicked as realised my plight. I was on a remote hill that would become my home for the next couple of weeks or however long it took. I was scared but I knew I could not back out now. I had to go through this. I could not fail. I was doing this to go free, to return to my family and be the man they needed me to be, to claim my place as head of the family and a man of honour in the community.

I recalled the way my father conducted himself and I felt ashamed. I had failed to become what he wanted of me. I was weak, ineffectual and indecisive, whereas he had been strong, decisive and with a high sense of morality. I was far removed from that and it hurt me.

That time I spent on the hill was one of the most amazing times of my life. I lived simply, sleeping when the sun set and waking when the sun rose. I meditated as much as I could and being by myself isolated I was able to really examine my life's wrongs. I was making progress towards eliminating the wrongs in my life. Releasing the hurt and pain made me happier. One day I experienced such an intense release that I was unable to move as I ascended into a deep feeling of peace that it remained with me for days. Was this it? Was I free now?

I remember there was flowing water near the tent. A small stream of water and I sat there watching it intensely, mesmerised by its beauty. The way the water flowed and how nature was fashioning this small stream. I would wash in this stream and sit by it and watch it. What a marvel. What a flow and what a beautiful creation it was.

One day I awoke to find myself looking at clouds barely a couple of feet away from me and I marvelled at being so close to them. I just watched until they dispersed, happy at having witnessed such beauty. Another day as I came out of my tent I saw a fawn not too far away from me and as I moved toward it, it would stop and as I stopped it would take a few steps. This dance between us continued for what seemed like an eternity until I tired of it and turned away.

I walked a lot too and there was a hill that I climbed several times a day. I felt alive and full of energy as I was healing. My simple diet and constant walking and the solitude of the place was renewing me, even the idea of going free was put aside as I marvelled every day at where I was and what was happening. Bliss! Days and nights blurred into one and time ceased to exist. I spoke to no one as no one was there. I was just in this perfect moment. No future, no past, just the moment. I just was and that was perfect.

I awoke in the middle of the night with an intense fear as if I was going to die, someone had screamed,

"I will kill you."

Someone was outside my tent and I felt the whole tent had been moved. I sensed I was in another part of the hill. I lay there paralysed by fear, no weapon with which to defend myself and convinced some maniac was outside. I lay there for what seemed like an eternity, waiting for the inevitable to happen. I knew I was going to be attacked, and had no means of dealing with it. I waited with baited breath. Muscles tightened, unable to move in fear. Any minute now I thought.

Then the thoughts dissipated into pure intense fear. I breathed deeply waiting for the attack. I waited and waited and when nothing happened I told myself to breathe, to release this feeling.

What was I without this feeling?

Could I let it go?

It is going, slowly but surely.

What am I without this feeling?

Could I let it go?

Slowly but surely I calmed down.

What had happened?

What was going on?

Where had that voice come from?

Was I going mad?

Was I hysterical?

Was I dead?

I resolved to get out of here at first light. I was shocked by my cowardice but convinced myself this was not the time for bravado. If someone had been out there I wasn't safe and if this was a trick of the mind well that was even scarier. Was this wanting to go free really worth it, if I was risking my very safety and sanity? In calm and rational retrospect I realised that I had not been very smart but rather blatantly stupid. Did I really think doing this was going to set me free? When was I going to learn?

After a tense night I rose and went down to the local village which was a couple of miles away to make some calls. When I returned I found a couple camped near me. I took this as a sign that it was time to leave this place and I was sad. I had failed again. I hadn't gone free and yet I wasn't as upset about this failure as I had expected. Maybe something had changed, something had been stirred. I spent that day climbing the hill and looking around at what had been my home for a few weeks. I looked at my tent with pride I had never owned property and this place had truly been my home, my simple way of living and yet I knew I had to go. Unknown to me something had changed leaving me with a glimmer of hope. I slept soundly that night having decided to stay another night within the forum of fear. It was however a peaceful and deep sleep.

I awoke late the next day to find the couple who had camped near me disappeared. It was a cold day and there were grey clouds and drizzle. I was sad to be going but I knew I had completed my time in exile from the world. I still felt fortunate for this experience to have escaped the world, to have tasted some semblance of freedom. I wondered if I would ever return, if I would ever share this secluded place with anyone.

I slowly dismantled the tent taking my time as I was lost in my thoughts weaving together my life's encounters, still attempting a conclusion. The silence around me confirmed that I was no longer the man who had arrived here. I needed to move on now.

I looked at the dismantled tent and knew I would never need it again and then I slowly started to break up the tent. No rage, no anger, nothing. I disposed of the tent into the dense overgrown bushes. I picked up my rucksack and walked down the hill. As I got to the bottom of the hill where I had made my home, I turned to give one final look and bade my farewell.

It's all an illusion...

I had returned to Coventry and had been here a number of months now and I was still searching, still finding and practicing alternate self-help methods. There was still an urgency to go free but a much more subdued one. I still felt at odds with my city and my family and I yearned to return to Scotland. I could not understand this desperate need to return to Scotland but anywhere was better than Coventry as far as I was concerned.

Honestly speaking it was not the city or people but more that I was reminded of my defeats and failures at every turn. I felt unheard as mental health illness was not acknowledged in the Asian community and especially amongst the elder generation. "Pull your socks up" was the typical attitude that was exhibited by my elders. I was drowning not waving and yet I remained ignored, unacknowledged.

The other debilitating fact about depression I found was that there was no one who could truly understand my plight, my pains. Well-meaning family and friends would talk to me and fill my mind with clichés after clichés bearing some truths but in that moment I was indifferent to everyone.

To anyone who is depressed reading this, understand that you will get better. Whilst I may sound clichéd and you may reject this with the counteracting thought of how I could possibly know the depth of your suffering? Consider this however that maybe there are people who understand and maybe if you reached out instead of wallowing in your self-pity then things could get better. Those well-meaning idiots who could not possibly know what you go through may just be the people who can help you. You are not alone and your unfounded belief in the fact that no one can know the depth of your suffering is killing you. So stop that.

At the time however I didn't realise this, so I felt alone in my suffering. I was still depressed and nothing worked and yet there was a glimmer of hope. I could run away to Scotland again but not to my hill. I could leave my suffering behind and make a fresh start, and that was exactly what I did.

Again the overnight journey, again switching off the phone and as I arrived in Glasgow I kept having Déjà vu's that I had done this before, I had been here before. That day I arranged a room unknown to me in one of Glasgow's most notorious hostels and as I entered the box room that was to become my home, a sense of even deeper depression blanketed me.

I awoke the next day to find the city covered in snow, there had been a freak snow storm. I ventured out simply because I couldn't stand to be in the room. Dressed in summer clothes, I was frozen within a few minutes of going out but anything was better than being in that room. I wandered over to a nearby café and had breakfast. This place would become my port of call every morning and the owner realising I was completely down and out would give me extra food, I was starting to see people could be nice, which was a refreshing change from years of being distrustful of people and totally paranoid. Life moved on and I moved with it.

"Come here you wee paki bastard!"

The man rushing towards me had a bottle in his hand and when I was able to decipher his thick Glaswegian accent and the words "Paki" and "Bastard" registered in my brain, I knew I was in trouble. I'd done martial arts and generally had a do not mess with me demeanour but this was not deterring the man and as the distance closed between us I could tell he was drunk.

For some strange reason I had offended him by being of brown skin and for that he fully intended to do me some harm. As he swung the bottle toward me, I stepped to the outside of his bottle carrying hand lowered my stance and pushed him, he toppled easily due to being drunk. As he fell he released the bottle and I heard it crash and break. I knew he had fallen badly but I had no intention of hanging around nor did the thought of finishing him off while he was down enter my head. I just let it be. I had done enough to be safe and I walked away swiftly.

I now knew that I was obviously a target for his attack because of my colour and I doubted this was the end of it. I needed to be out of the hostel. I had not arrived in this city to get chibbed (slashed with a knife or bottle) as the locals said.

I was able to secure my own accommodation within days of the incident and moved into my own place, a one bedroom flat on Glasgow's Southside. It looked like a throwback to the seventies. I had a lounge with a bedroom/kitchen area. There was also what could only be described as a very small room which could have doubled up as a walk in wardrobe and I was informed that in days of old this is where people slept in the harsh Glaswegian winters.

So here I was with my own flat. I had some clothes and that was it. None of the luxuries of modern life were here. I had no television, DVD, laptop or anything resembling modern life and I was all alone.

This seclusion I found myself in was not my creation just like the time in the highlands. It had happened naturally. I spent my time thinking and walking, always constantly asking myself what had gone wrong in my life and what I wanted in my life. I quickly realised in this situation I could devote myself to seeking truth and freedom as I was in a financial position to do so. I lived simply and had minimal outgoings so I threw myself into seeking as one would a full time occupation. It was around this time that I remembered the speaker.

The phone rang and the man answered, I had seen his picture and his writings on the internet and had found a contact number for him so decided to call him. I had previously spoken to him for about thirty seconds the year before and he had returned to my thoughts. After the initial pleasantries and introductions I asked my first question,

"What's this all about?"

The answer which came back stunned me into silence.

"If you think this will improve your life, it won't", He replied.

I remember the life draining from me as I continued to listen, knowing that what I was hearing was destroying all I had ever known. Was this the truth I sought because all I knew was that my brain was exploding and after what seemed like an eternity the call ended. I thanked the speaker and he replied that I could phone him whenever I wanted. I felt drained and tired and not liking what I had heard. I was angry and confused but I decided to put this out my mind.

The following Sunday I rang the speaker again and this became my routine. Every Sunday I would ring the speaker and he would talk to me. Something was changing. I was resonating with the message he was presenting and after our calls I would go for long walks thinking about what I had heard and assimilating what I had heard. The primary message I was hearing was the mind could not know this and yet all I had was my mind to make sense of this. Allied to this the message said this was all an illusion and yet my pain, suffering and life felt very real. I disagreed with some aspects of what he was saying, especially that there was nothing I could do to be free and yet I continued phoning and talking. One day after a call the speaker made the following statement,

"One day you will ring me and say I understand that which can't be spoken of"

I thanked him, hoping that I would one day attain what he spoke of, even though I now knew there was nothing I could do to be free according to the speaker.

"Don't think too much"

My friend had said. I smiled

"I won't". I replied

I'd gone to the railway station to drop off my friend who was off to Cardiff to see family. My friend was fully aware of my seeking and worried that with all this searching and thinking that I would go mad. Her concerns were justified given the depths of my depression.

I was back at my flat, alone as per usual. I had just returned from the railway station and it was getting late. I toyed with the idea of going on another walk, the umpteenth of the day but settled on going to bed instead. It had been a long day and I was really tired. I decided instead to go to bed and call it day. I had previously always had trouble sleeping but in those last couple of months the walking and thinking resulted in me becoming fitter and having much more restful sleep. I was literally getting into bed shattered every night. This night was no different and as my head hit the pillow, I was out like a light.

I awoke the next day and immediately the first thought that hit me like a hammer was,

I'm no longer depressed!

Hold on I thought to myself this can't be right. I'm no longer depressed. I tried to find some semblance of depression in me. Surely it must be still there, it had been my constant companion for years and I had tired of it, wallowed in it, used it as an excuse and gone into the depths of madness with it and now it wasn't here. This wasn't right; where was it? After a while I realised it really was gone. I was done with depression, my constant companion had gone. That voice in my head which had destroyed any semblance of sanity in my life which had sapped my energy and drained the very life out of me was gone. I felt different somehow as if a huge burden had been lifted. I felt free and light. The weight that for so long had held me down was now gone. I could move on.

To this day I do not know how my depression went or if I had done something to let it go. Maybe all the walking, thinking or meditation in the past had somehow shifted me. I really could not say all I knew was that I was free of it. Even challenging situations now which in the past would have resulted in the heavy fog of depression coming down on me were gone. It has never returned and I am free of it.

If you are depressed know there is a way out of it. You are not some story or thought that is repetitively going around your head. What you are is so much more. You need to trust yourself that you can be rid of this debilitating condition. Be gentle with yourself and have hope that matters will improve. I had always fought my depression as I knew that had I not I would be dead. It had once before taken me to the doors of death with a failed suicide attempt and I did not want to go back. At that time the hope that I would be free was almost a flicker, a flame ready to be extinguished and yet I came back from some very dark times.

Know this; you are powerful and strong beyond measure. Your mind has such strong thoughts as to bring you to your knees. Don't beat yourself up about it. Instead realise that if you can go into this downward spiral then you can surely moment by moment and thought by thought turn the spiral in the other direction. Slowly but surely. Rome was not built in a day and nor will you just pop free of depression. I know it may sound like I did but maybe there was a culmination of thoughts that led to it. Sometimes even when we think we are not changing we are. In an ideal world maybe we could look at ourselves objectively step outside ourselves but we do not have that ability yet. Know this, do your best, have hope. It can improve. Others go free of this and so can you.

This indeed was a huge shift I was now no longer depressed. Again something was shifting but I was still so fixated on trying to go free that this momentous event in my life would only truly be appreciated years later. Had I realised that if I was able to overcome depression then I was able to limitlessly achieve much more, maybe my journey to going free could have been drastically shortened. At the time however the urge to go free restricted me from truly appreciating the changes I was going through and I continued seeking.

One day in a fit of desperation I walked fifteen miles to Loch Lomond and climbed to the top of a hill. I told myself I would achieve this even if it killed me and I stood there at the top of the hill and stretched out my arms.

"I accept you!"

In my despair I was doing anything I could to go free of this suffering. Trying any nonsensical thing I could so desperate to go free that sense and reason had been left at the door.

"I accept you!"

Nothing

"I accept you!"

Silence

"I accept"

Emptiness

"I"

I have failed again.

It was getting dark and I was on top of the hill, arms outstretched. This was stupid I wasn't getting this. Rage, anger and a feeling of foolishness welled up in me. This was pathetic, when was I going to learn?

I found a country railway station on the way back; there was no way I was walking back. I got on the train and sat there silently. I arrived in Glasgow and went to my local takeaway bought some food and returned to my flat. I ate, locked up and went to sleep. I was done and if anyone mentioned freedom to me, I would have killed them. It was over.

I awoke the next day, the previous day's events came to mind and I winced at my latest defeat. I no longer wanted to know I had no more desire to go free. Let's face it I was a loser and this was just another loss, albeit a very painful one. Who was I too think I could achieve something that billions before me had tried and failed at. Who did I think I was? I wasn't special I was just a guy losing at life. It wasn't worth it anymore I would be better off just getting on with the life I had, but what did I have? I had a life on benefits I was at the lowest rung of society and I had nothing. It was almost as if I didn't really exist. I didn't have a loving relationship, a house, a car, credit cards, a bank balance, a decent job or business. By the barometers of success that were used by my community I was an out and out failure.

I didn't need to be thinking about this anymore. I decided to numb myself to this latest failure by forgetting it had happened. I was good at that, blotting out whatever failed to serve my purpose or my other favourite, blaming everyone but me.

The next couple of days were spent just living my life. Get up, go out, buy food, do some reading and go for walks simple nothing more or less. I just got on with my day to day life. I liked this, I was in a city where no one knew me my family did not know my whereabouts. No one really knew who I was. As I walked down the street I realised I enjoyed this anonymity. I did not exist I was just another person going through life and I had this freedom to be whatever I chose to.

I remember once watching a film about a writer who fantasised he was someone else. Well I could be that person an international arms dealer a spy or one of the jet set. I had without realising it at that moment in my life, no responsibility, no ties, nothing. I was master of my destiny. This was good and this scenario made me totally forget my troubles. I continued over the next couple of days to play with different scenarios. One day I was an international man of mystery, albeit a very poor one but a man of mystery indeed.

I was though slowly without realising it starting to return into life. Previously I had nothing but now I had a little flat, slowly but surely things were changing. I was so caught up in wanting to go free that I failed to see that I was starting to slowly change. Ever since falling down, I had been starting to rise again. This is something most seekers on the path fail to see, that they are always travelling towards improving.

Like myself however they are sometimes so fixated on the end goal, they feel they are going nowhere and beat themselves up about it as I was doing. I had beaten my depression and yet such an amazing incident in my life never received the acknowledgement it deserved. I was changing and yet I was blinded to the changes. This though at that moment in my life was the furthest thing from my mind I was failing and also failing to count my blessings and all that was good in my life.

It was a Sunday morning and I awoke early. I had forgotten to draw the curtains and the light shone through the window. It was a beautiful day and I thought about going out for a walk but the bed was too nice and warm. I lay there for what felt an eternity thinking about nothing in particular. I spied a plane in the distant sky and my eyes followed it and its vapour trail. Who was on board? Where was it travelling too? Would I one day travel on a plane to some far off place? Questions rose and fell in my mind.

Finally my hunger persuaded me to leave the bed and I headed towards the kitchen. The floor felt cold to the touch and yet nice due to the flat being really hot. I hastily made a cup of tea and headed toward the armchair I liked to sit in. I knew it was a big day today. World Cup final today, Italy was playing France. I did not possess a television and had no real desire to watch the match. I sat in the armchair content to be having a cup of tea and thinking about nothing in particular.

I surveyed my flat and thought it was really funny that I had my own flat now, for a guy who a couple of years earlier struggled to function properly. I now had a flat. This was nice. Little chores like going shopping and paying bills that most people take for granted that I had never done because I was so obsessed with going free I now found amazing. Just to go shopping, pay bills, balance my chequebook and do 'normal' things felt like after all these years I was starting to grow up.

I was unusually optimistic about my life. Maybe if this carried on I could save up some money and buy my own place, meet someone and settle down, but I thought that was somewhere in the future and it felt too complicated so I was happy to just enjoy what I had.

My thoughts turned once again to wanting to be free and I winced at the last attempt to go free but as it was such a beautiful day I was happy to let myself entertain these thoughts of going free. Sure it had been a crazy couple of years and I had done some things that others would consider insane but I suppose I just had to go through it. Yet here I was in my little flat, in a beautiful city doing something that most people would never do, trying to go free.

In that sense this was cool and I smiled to myself. Wow I thought a smile on a face that had learned not to smile, surely that must be something. Once again I went back into my thoughts and as thoughts raced through my mind, something stirred. I looked up and noticed the ironing board and I felt an intense feeling that remains indescribable. Oh my god I thought.

"This is it", I said aloud to no one in particular,

I was aware of what was happening,

I was it,

I was witnessing it,

I knew it,

It knew me,

It was me,

I was it,

I am FREE,

And in that instant Zahir woke up from the dream of life.

It was done I was free. It was ten past two in the afternoon. France was playing Italy in the World Cup final and in some nondescript flat in a nondescript street in Glasgow I had finally woken up from the dream of life. It was over. I was done.

I sat there silently, I was different, something had changed, and unlike other changes this was different. I continued sitting there, no thoughts nothing. I just sat. Only one thing came up I was tired, tired as if I had been travelling for years and now I had arrived at my destination. Now I was here! I rose and walked back to my bedroom. I put on some music and listened to it until I fell asleep. It was done, I was home.

I woke up the next day and the first thing I noticed was that the feeling of having woken up from this play of life, spiritual awakening or whatever you want to call it was still there. I was free, enlightened, done. I changed and went for a walk, everything felt new and so much more intense. I noticed I seemed to have a permanent smile on my face and this continued for days. I wandered the streets of Glasgow, happy and alive, smiling at people. Matters that confused me before made sense. I was just happy and everything was good. I would just occasionally while walking just stop and observe simple things, but now they were awe inspiring. There was nothing but this freedom. Nothing else mattered. I had no desire to talk of it, analyse it or even do anything with it. I was free, yes I was finally free and it felt amazing. Days went on in this amazing blissed out state and now I had achieved my goal it was time for me to go back into life. Wow I thought I have woken up.

I found a job in a small publishing company and happily settled into the routine of work. I phoned the speaker whom I had never met, recounted my experiences and was invited to a meeting in London to share my experience. I agreed to go. So I took an overnight coach and found myself in London a week later. I first went to the Kew Greenhouse Coffee shop, my favourite coffee shop in London. I had been here many a time when I was depressed or needed to escape but as I sat there this time I couldn't help but smile as this time I was free, I was truly free. I was so enjoying myself. Life was working and I glided through life without any hint of effort, worry or anything. I seemed to have a permanent smile on my face and I felt changed. I was different and now here I was in the big city of London being asked to share my experience. I had time and so I went to Hyde Park and then made my way to the meeting to meet the speaker.

"Alright mate you're the speaker aren't you". I said

"Yes I am who are you?" He replied.

"I'm Zahir we spoke on the phone".

The speaker smiled and leaned forward and gave me a huge hug, as he did so, his wife walked past and he excitedly turned to her,

"This is Zahir, the guy I told you about".

She beamed a huge smile at me and hugged me too, how lovely where these two amazing people.

We talked for a while and the speaker said;

"No pressure, but if you would like to share that would be lovely, if you don't that's fine too; it is as it is". He smiled and then turned and went.

I entered the hall there must have been at least one hundred and fifty people there, some I recognised as other speakers whose sites I had visited. I sat next to an old lady who asked me where I had come from and was pleasantly shocked when I told her I had travelled from Scotland. She was a lovely elderly white lady from Wales with an Indian name. When I asked her to explain she stated she had lived in an ashram in India in the seventies with a guru and he had given her this name. Indeed most of the crowd were affluent middle to upper middle class who all appeared very knowledgeable about spiritual matters. I felt slightly nervous about sharing, what could I say that most of these clearly intellectual and spiritual types had not heard before?

The speaker entered and a hush descended on the crowd. He sat at the head of the room everyone craned forward and after an uncomfortably long silence he spoke,

"All there is, is this".

The talk settled into a pattern of the speaker speaking and different people asking questions interspersed with long silences. I listened intently it all made sense and I felt happy. It was at this point the speaker said something and just looked at me, not a prompt or anything, he just looked at me and I found myself saying,

"Yes, that's right for whether you're seeking or not seeking you are it, so whether you were here or not, all there is, is freedom".

"Steady on", said the speaker with a huge smile,

"That's bad for business".

The crowd roared with laughter. It was time for a break and for tea and biscuits.

As I had never shared this before I sought out the speaker.

"Was that ok, I didn't say anything wrong did I?" I asked.

"No, it was perfect" and he smiled at me.

I smiled and then met a few more people who wanted to talk to me and I exchanged phone numbers and email addresses with some people who had heard me share my experience. I even spoke to a few and it was fun. I talked to a few other speakers and then returned to the talk. The rest of the talk was fun and at the end I met the speaker and his wife who thanked me for coming and both gave me a huge hug. What a lovely day I thought even though the day was not finished yet.

Afterwards I met some friends in Camden Town and had dinner and then we headed to Birmingham. That night lying on my friend's couch I experienced an even deeper release and my awakening deepened. The next day I went back up to Glasgow happy and content. Life was good and no doubt it would get better.

Over the coming months I did a few talks in Glasgow, a couple of people came and I found that two things happened. Firstly I talked nothing like the speaker and this concerned me as I wanted to sound very clear in my communication and I seemed to be going into areas such as Sufism and other approaches in my talks. This was a cause for concern for me and I stopped talking and then something even worse happened.

I awoke one morning and something felt different it was as if something had left and I realised that my worst nightmare had come true. I felt different and it felt as if someone had pulled the rug from underneath me. The only way to describe it was I had lost my awakening, my enlightenment. This was horrible and I was petrified by this development.

For days I thought about nothing else and my work suffered too. I did not think to call anyone and instead went deeper into my thoughts. Around this time I remembered one of the speakers I had met at the London talk, so I resolved to meet him and ask him what was going on. I made another trip to London.

The person who opened the door to me was a middle aged man, trim and athletic. We were meeting at his flat in North London. He was a practitioner of the Feldenkrais system and also talked about Enlightenment. We sat in the room where he conducted talks and I relayed what had happened to me and he offered a simple explanation,

"Sometimes we awaken and after a while the mind returns, the personality returns. This really is the last vestiges of the mind trying to keep hold of its existence. It will keep reasserting itself until it is no more and then there is just liberation".

We spoke for an hour and I listened intently to his answers. So I wasn't completely free and yet the strange thing was I was kind of ok with it at the moment. Yes I still wanted to go totally free, liberated and yet I was kind of ok with the state of affairs that I was in. My old self wouldn't have been too pleased but I was more determined now than before to succeed but not so desperate about it. We talked further and when it was time for me to go, I thanked him for his time and left the flat to return to Scotland.

I entered my little flat and felt that I should move on from here too. The flat had no double glazing and was bitterly cold in the winter. I had offered to pay more rent if the landlord would install double glazing but the landlord had refused. It was too much of a capital outlay and so I made the decision to move into another flat. I was sad to leave as I had such wonderful times there but I comforted myself by viewing it as a new start.

The new flat turned out to be a total disaster it was unfurnished. I had intended to furnish it but something about this flat failed to resonate with me so I ended up leaving it as it was and slept on the floor. It just did not have the same feel as my old flat.

I also had several fallings out with the friend who had helped me to find my hill when I had first arrived in Glasgow and with her becoming a victim of black magic after returning from a trip to India. Our friendship ended in an argument one day when I suggested she was under the influence of black magic. She was my closest friend in Glasgow and I had come to really care for her. Seeing as we were no longer talking and I was really just by myself in Glasgow I felt it was time to move on. I was heartbroken to be leaving. I felt I was being kicked out of the city I had come to love. I was going back home and as far as I was concerned not returning.

I was on the road again with nowhere to go. I decided to pay a visit to an old school friend and ended up staying on his couch for a few months. I was though occasionally going up to Scotland to see friends and each visit would remind me of my desire to be free but I had reached a point where I was able to bury the idea away. Life was taking on another colour and I was more interested in making money then pursuing grandiose but impractical ideas such as going free.

I thought about it one day, how much time I had wasted in trying to go free when I could have just been trying to sort my life out. Found a job, a house, a car and been responsible. My present life was miles away from this image and I was starting to see that it was wrong. I also wanted to start a family and just settle down but again the nature of my existence was such that it was not possible. I had nothing to offer any potential partner. I was really stuck in a rut. I had to choose between carrying on pursuing freedom or letting it all go and settling down and having a normal life. I was at a crossroads.

My decision would be made for me one morning when I awoke and decided to go to my hometown of Coventry. Driving down I sensed something was happening to me. I couldn't figure it out but I felt I was falling apart. It was an odd sensation as nothing seemed like it was happening yet there was intensity in the moment. It was an uncomfortable sensation as if something was being pulled apart. Jung talked of the dark night of the soul. Could I be going through this? I asked my old school friend to drop me off at the local Masjid. I had one man in mind that I needed to speak to and he was the Imam of the local Masjid.

I walked towards the Masjid. It was a hot day and I was sweating profusely. I was having trouble seeing and my eyes were blood red. My mind was swirling with a million thoughts, none of which I could recognise or stop and I felt an energy swell up in me and yet I was tired. I knew that in my present state I was going to do something stupid. Maybe walk into the Masjid and start arguing with someone or say something totally ecstatic causing myself to be beaten up. I wanted a fight, I wanted to die I wanted blood. I was a crazed man looking to cause trouble. To walk into a place of God and to tell them they were wrong. I wanted trouble and I was going to find it. The site of a funeral cortege outside the Masjid made me temporarily come to my senses and I resolved to see the Imam when I could.

I have no idea how but I arrived home and told my mother I was here for a fleeting visit. She was still under the impression that I lived in Glasgow. I was however twenty miles away on my friends couch but I decided not to tell her this. I ate and chatted to my mother, brother and sisters and then went to bed.

I awoke the next day and went downstairs looking like some wild banshee having not shaved. I looked rough! My mother had some religious channel on and as I ate my breakfast I watched the speaker. All of a sudden I started laughing and simultaneously crying. It really was a strange sensation and I remember my focus being the speaker on the screen not on what he was saying but instead on him. I felt like everything I was going through was making sense on some level and yet on another level nothing was making sense. It was just mad and yet it was a madness that made sense and that was stopping me from dropping off the edge. My mother as you can imagine was alarmed and concerned by my behaviour. I turned to her,

"I need to see the Imam".

She nodded

"Ok, I know his wife we will go now".

I could tell she was thinking is my son possessed or going mad? Hastily she made a call to the Imams wife to tell her we needed to see her husband.

To this day I will never know why I chose that particular Imam.

I have no idea why I felt it was so necessary to see him.

We walked to his house, me in this engulfing madness combined with a feeling of being powerful and strong. In the throes of ecstasy, here I was whirling like a dervish, simultaneously alive and dead. We arrived at the Imams house and I immediately went on the offensive.

"I am everything; there is no separation in me". I stated.

The Imam looked at me and started talking, to this day I don't know what he was saying but everything he was saying I was dismissing and batting away.

"I'm trying to tell you something". I said aggressively.

The Imam listened and then went over to the bookshelf and brought back a copy of the Holy Quran. I needed to let him know what was happening to me now. Verse after verse he read to see if it fit my condition and each time I would reply no, not this one. This went on for a few hours and then I looked at him.

"I need to tell you something".

"Tell me" he replied with a smile.

I narrated to him a dream I had and as I did tears welled up and I cried uncontrollably. The Imam smiled and looked over at my concerned mother.

"You do not need to worry about him, he is going to be fine", he said and smiled again.

"Pray for me", I cried between tears and the Imam raised his hands and we prayed together.

The Imam came to my house the next day and brought with him his Quran, again we went through different verses. At the end we settled upon a verse which described what was happening to me. The Imam prayed for me once more and as he left the house he turned to me and smiled and then said something I will never forgot.

"The work of years will happen in days", and with that he was gone.

I decided to stay in Coventry and the summer took on a familiar pattern. I would rise and go see the Imam and we would talk. These were amazing meetings and much was shared and talked of, at times the Imam or I would say something and the other would just go into an ecstatic feeling that I had never encountered before.

I reacquainted myself with old friends who were now part of a different Sufi school. One friend took me along to a Sufi group and I would go there every Thursday nights. I became a local at the Masjid and became part of the Masjid crowd, because of my earlier awakening I would talk and soon there was a small gang of us. We would talk until the early hours of the morning and I spent that summer meeting other Sufis and going to different gatherings. Around this time I started feeling a sensation around my heart region as if something ached. I was suitably informed that the heart was awakening and that it was a good thing. I was invited by my Sufi friends to meet their master in Cyprus but I was unable to accept as enough was happening in Coventry without travelling to Cyprus.

One day I went to the Masjid to perform Friday prayers and when the prayers were ending I started to cry tears streamed down my face and people in the crowd started to notice. I could not control what was happening and I sobbed hysterically. I walked toward the Imam still crying but he smiled at me and asked,

"How are you?"

I looked at him for a few seconds and said in desperation,

"I'm falling apart!"

He smiled and raised his hands and replied

"Say Alhamdulillah" (praise be to Allah)

I wept and wept, was this pain never to leave me. I needed to be free and I was nowhere near my goal. Life moved on.

The phone rang and I let it ring, it was late afternoon and I'd been in bed having a nap. I looked at the caller identification it was a dear friend.

"Salaam Alaikum brother" I answered.

"Walaikum Salaam Brother, how's you? Listen we are going to Cardiff tonight to a big Sufi gathering and the son of the grandmaster will be there. You're coming brother because a few of the brothers are going and I need someone sane with me".

I knew exactly what he meant some of the brothers were a bit far out and zealous in their pursuit of the goal. These Sufis made me look positively tame and I shared my friends concerns too. We had been friends for years ever since we had met in a library and we had shared many an adventure on the spiritual path, so much so that we were almost a double act, so it figured where I went he would too and where he went I would too.

"Yeah sure brother, why not" I replied

"Cool be there in ten then" he said.

I laughed at the fact that he had already made plans having decided I was going so maybe it would have been better if he had just arrived and opened the car door and bundled me in.

As promised ten minutes later the car arrived with two other brothers and my friend and I were off to Cardiff. The gathering we were going too was being held by students from the same school as my ex teacher, albeit another branch of them. The man presiding over the meeting was the son who had taken over the school when his father the Grandshaykh had passed on.

At one time this man and my ex teacher had been students together. This brought up a myriad of feelings, it was like going back but not quite. I had not seen this school for many years and part of me wanted to talk to the man who was now the new master and ask him why they had allowed our ex teacher to get away with the things he had done. Three out of the four of us in this car had been students of the ex-teacher each with their own story to tell and although the other two were a little more philosophical about it I wasn't so forgiving now and resolved to ask this current master what he was doing about his old fellow student.

The scene that greeted us in the hall was awash with colour and bodies, Sufis whirled and the flags of different colours had been hoisted above everyone, each representing the different Sufi schools who had gathered into this school. The logic being that this school now received spiritual power from all the different schools and hence was the most powerful of schools. My friend and the brothers went to see the master and kissed his hands and bowed to him. I however hung back as I had no intention of kissing this man's hand. As each moment progressed and the whirling continued I started to feel more and more agitated, angrier and less appreciative of what was happening.

The master noticed this and looked in my direction a few times disapprovingly. I was observed by a few of the master's students for my odd behaviour. I even refused to greet the master. This was out of character for me as I am usually polite but at that moment all I wanted to do was cause trouble.

A Khalifah of the master came up to me, a Khalifah is one given permission to teach and as this ocean of calm came up to me, my friend hurried on over. My friend was aware that I could become unreasonable and sarcastic at such gatherings asking stupid questions and generally pouring scorn on the schools methods. He therefore hurried over just as the Khalifah approached me.

"Brother are you alright". He asked

"Taking in the theatrics", I replied

My friend winced; it was going to be a long night as far as he was concerned.

"What do you mean by this?" The Khalifah asked.

"Look at it" I shot back. "This is all a joke, you guys haven't got a clue and you're here misleading others". I mentioned the ex-teachers name and asked what they were doing about a man who was abusing pupils in the name of this school.

"Allah will punish him", replied the Khalifah.

"Yeah Allah will punish him but how many more students will be sexually abused or taken in by this charlatan until then?" I asked.

The Khalifah looked at me. I think he realised he could not say anything that would have any effect on me. I on the other hand kept peppering him with questions.

My friend tried to interject but I was on a roll and I was becoming angry. I started showering him with questions each designed to elicit a response a reaction. To his credit he stayed calm and answered my questions.

My friend who had been watching this tried to lead me away and asked the Khalifah to help me as I was going through some hard times spiritually. At this comment I lost it.

I loudly swore at him.

"What can this fucking idiot do, he hasn't got a fucking clue" I screamed.

People stopped and my friend bundled me out of there. We returned to the car whilst I continued to rant and rave. I was angry with everything and everyone. I was angry with the world and those in my immediate vicinity became subjects of my anger. I continued swearing and ranting.

One of the brothers asked me to stop swearing and he received mouthful of abuse from me. Another brother, my senior from the old school started speaking and his quiet voice with reasoned measured words brought to me a calm and peace I had been missing for a long time. I do not recall much of what he said but it made sense and I loved him for it.

I was suffering in this separation and this man who had over the years continued to be there for me was saying things which now made sense. He did not ask me to accept anything but as he spoke I went calm and sat in silence listening to what could only be described as a simple wisdom. The couple of hours we travelled together stretched into an eternity as he my senior brother spoke. A simple beautiful discourse, spoken by a man whose beauty it reflected.

In the Garden again...

A few days after the incident in Cardiff I decided to return to my flat in Scotland to help my friend who was returning from India and appeared to still have an issue with black magic. I began my journey I was fearful yet excited about what I knew deep down would happen. I was oblivious to how I would help her all I knew was that that I needed to help her.

Black magic is a huge issue in the Asian community and many a life has been ruined by it. I myself had been a victim of it and as cynical as I was about such matters when I had realised something was wrong and felt compelled to seek help but before I sought help came to me.

My mother's friend was visiting and on seeing me she had remarked that someone had cast the evil eye upon me. She had further added that my mother was not to say anything to me and that I would reveal this to my mother myself. The next day I did indeed tell my mother that I felt something was really wrong in my life and it may be black magic.

There had followed months of pain as I prayed and drank holy water and generally questioned my existence and sanity. At one point in the depths of despair I had turned against the old lady helping me and accused her of doing this to me. She had remained silent as no doubt she had seen this behaviour before but she continued to help me and disappeared out of my life after helping me so I was never able to thank her. I wish I had been given the opportunity; she truly was an amazing soul.

It was due to my experience that I was keen to help my friend. When I reflect on this episode however there were two things I found very strange. One was the experience itself and secondly the end result. As I have said I had no idea how I was going to figure this out.

I arrived in Glasgow and was met by a woman who would become pivotal to me in the coming months. She was a single mother and had come across me from a talk I did several months ago. Whilst she did not attend she had taken my number from the poster and rung me. I realised after several conversations with her that her problems were above me and I was out my depth but I agreed to meet her.

The woman was unlike anyone I had ever met. She was in her early thirties and had six children, one of whom was severely disabled. As I heard her story I realised that my troubles were a blessing in comparison to hers. As she narrated her story I became determined to help her as much as I could. I agreed she could come and talk to me and for the next couple of months she came to my flat and listened intently as I spoke and shared my ideas and views. She never commented and just listened. Occasionally she would bring food for me and I was invited to meet her children. They were a beautiful set of children and a real credit to her and yet I noticed that each was oblivious to the suffering of their mother, and around them she concealed her pain.

Whilst certain clues revealed her pain they were only noticeable to those who knew what to look for. Many people did not know her pain. She in time became a good friend and I learnt as much from her as she learnt from me. We have since then lost contact but her story has a happy ending as she finally discovered what was good in her life and moved forward in a really positive way. Wherever she is now I know she is well and is a true friend.

I settled back into life in Glasgow. The flat was sorted out, friends were informed I was back and then I had a thought that I should contact the speaker again. It had been a year since we last talked during my attendance at one of his lectures. It would be good to talk and catch up.

The phone rang and I heard the familiar voice of the speaker. After the initial greetings we soon settled into our conversation and I asked questions and the speaker answered. It was then that it happened. We were talking and all sense of self just disappeared. I was intensely in the moment. Nothing mattered apart from the moment. The very act of holding a phone to my ear was all there was. This was it. I recognised this from before and I tried to speak but found myself at a loss of words. The speaker sensing this laughed over the phone. All there was this very moment. Nothing else mattered. This moment was the sum total of my existence and that was it. I tried to speak again to verbalise what I felt but heard myself saying "It's like, it's like, and it's like". I truly was at a loss for words. I was totally in the moment and that was it.

The speaker sensed what was happening and allowed me the time I needed to "return to earth" so as to speak. Eventually after what appeared an eternity, some semblance of me returned and I thanked the speaker for our conversation. He asked if I would like to come down again and share my experience. I agreed, this was unlike anything before and all I felt was love. We said our goodbyes and I found myself alone in my flat. There was a difference though; I was back in the garden again.

Life again turned into a blissful experience. I once again went to London and met the speaker and his wife. Once again I spoke, a little bit longer this time but what was funny was the reaction from the woman next to me. She had been sat there taking notes furiously and when I spoke her mouth literally dropped open.

"Wow, are you a liberated being?"

I simply smiled. I was in a state of intense bliss. The rest of the talk was a joyous outpouring of love and I felt like I was on cloud nine. The talk came to an end and I walked up to the speaker. We hugged and he thanked me for coming to share. There was a group of people waiting for the speaker to sign their books and we looked over at this group.

"Oh my god, I'm famous", joked the speaker and we laughed.

The speaker accompanied me to the door where he was joined by his wife. I said my goodbyes and hugged the speaker again and I also hugged his lovely wife. I started to walk away but as I got to the end of the hall I was compelled to turn around and I saw the speaker and his wife in a loving embrace, holding each other and looking deeply into each other's eyes. I smiled at this beautiful scene and walked out the door.

The next month and a half saw me in a total state of bliss, everything worked. I never worked yet money came to me regularly. I never cooked and yet food came to me. My life became a simple existence and I drifted through days in a total state of bliss. Life worked and as far as I was concerned this was it. I was finally free. I had finally attained my goal.

I moved out of my flat and into a new flat and started working out and praying. I would pray five times a day and in the evenings visit the local Masjid and pray there. There was a group of regulars who would pray there; they were mostly old men and I became friends with them. After prayers they would sit and I would join them with my prayer beads and listen to them speaking about their lives and their journeys on the Islamic path.

For me this was an amazing time and I drifted through life with no rhyme or reason. At long last things started to work for me and I saw light at the end of what had been a very long dark tunnel. One day I went to the masjid to pray. It had been an incredible day and I was feeling unusually ecstatic. As I prayed all sense of time and space disappeared and all that was left was the act of prayer. As I stood, kneeled, sat and bowed in the prayer there was just the prayer. With each prayer and each passing moment I went deeper and deeper into love. There was only this prayer, nothing else and then a thought arose.

"Who am I praying too, am I praying to myself?"

The gravity of the thought shattered everything and I stood stunned. The thought circled and I kept asking "who am I praying too? To whom am I praying"? The feeling was such that I struggled to finish my prayer and when it was done I sat quietly. In the silence I realised something had happened. I had spent day and night in this bliss and was sure I was done but I was not.

That one thought had shattered my bliss and once again I was thrown out of the garden. Sure I could find some semblance of bliss but the question, who am I praying to had ended it. Unknown to me at that time my second awakening had just finished. What was to come next would question my very existence.

My friend returned from India and there began for me several months of madness. It was around this time I met two Sufis, one a Shaykh and one I would consider a Faqir, both pivotal in changing my life. One was of the Naqshbandi School and was the man who helped me fight the magic. I had heard of him over the years from friends in Coventry but had never met him in person.

Matters became crazy in Glasgow with my friend denying that any such magic had happened to her. I would remind her of the black knots that had been sewn into a shirt she had shown me earlier. She would however become all distant and argumentative, it was after one such argument that I phoned a friend from Coventry and demanded the number of the Shaykh.

Surprisingly he handed over the phone and address with no argument.

I got ready and headed towards the railway station and bought a ticket to Rochdale.

"You're lucky mate the train is ten minutes late so that's saved you waiting for the next train", said the man in the ticket office.

I boarded the train, a million thoughts in my head as to why everything was happening the way it was. Things were definitely not right and I had to get to the bottom of this.

I arrived in Manchester where the connecting train to Rochdale was also ten minutes late, meaning I caught that too instead of missing it and I arrived some twenty minutes later in the hometown of the Shaykh that I had for years doubted existed.

The street the Shaykh lived on was a typical street to be found in the north consisting of row upon row of terraced houses. I wondered if I was on the right path. I was expecting a master of all ages to live in something a bit more than this. I knocked on the door and waited.

"What do you want?"

I looked up to see a man looking out at me from the top window. His appearance was Middle Eastern and I gathered he must be a student of the Shaykh.

"I'd like to see the Shaykh", I replied. At this point my phone rang and it was my friend from Coventry asking if I had arrived there. I gestured for the student to wait as I finished my conversation with my friend. I reverted to the man and he asked why I needed to see the Shaykh. I replied that I had a problem and it was important for me to speak to him. He studied my face and then shut the window and was gone.

I was not very happy with his dismissive manner and silently swore under my breath.

I knocked on the door a few times and nothing, even the student did not come out again. I became impatient and angry. Who was this idiot of a student who had just shut the window on me? As I stood there it started raining heavily and I found myself drenched as I unsuccessfully attempted to take shelter in the doorway. I therefore contacted the brother who organised the weekly Zikr class in Coventry and who was a good friend of the Shaykh for assistance.

"Salaam Alaikum", he answered.

"Walaikum salaam", I replied.

"How can I help you brother?" he asked.

"Brother I am in Rochdale at the Shaykh's. I just knocked on the door and some student of his asked me who I was and brother my phone went off and I wasn't able to talk to him properly. I may have offended him, anyways now no one is opening the door, I think the Shaykh has done one and disappeared out of there, maybe he used his powers to vanish?" I said half-jokingly.

The brother laughed.

"Or maybe he just went out of the back door?"

Did I feel stupid? That one comment summed up my life back then, signs, superstitions and a distorted outlook on life.

"Look do this, there is a little restaurant around the corner go there dry yourself off and have some food and write the Shaykh a letter, apologise if you feel you have caused offense, tell them in the letter why you are here and leave your phone number in it", said the brother.

"Ok sounds like the right thing to do, thanks brother", I replied.

I put down the phone and went to the restaurant where I ate and composed my note, careful to sound very apologetic and reverential. I went back to the house and posted it through the letterbox and decided to head to the railway station and wait. I decided that if there was no response I would return to Manchester and stay there for a night and revisit the next day and keep coming back until he saw me. I was determined to meet the Shaykh.

An hour passed by and nothing, two hours and still nothing, time ticked by and nothing, maybe I was wrong. The Shaykh was not obligated to see me. I did not even belong to his school and I did not even believe in teachers. I was of the opinion that it was all an illusion and I was what I sought. I had even awoken without a teacher so why was I here? As these thoughts swirled through my mind daylight turned into darkness and I decided to return to Manchester and at least sort my accommodation out for the night. I headed towards the platform and it was then that my phone rang.

"Salaam Alaikum you wish to see me", the voice asked.

"Yes, I have a problem", I replied.

"You are not going to go away until I see you are you?" He asked.

"No I'm not; I'll keep coming back until you see me". I replied shocked at my boldness.

The voice chuckled,

"Ok there is a car coming for you in five minutes".

The line went dead, wow I had just spoken to the Shaykh this man whom I was fast coming to the conclusion did not even exist. I had heard of him but never seen him and now I had just spoken to him and I was finally going to meet him. I hastily made my way to the front of the station to see a customised car pulling up being driven by a young man playing really loud dance music. He wound the window down,

"Yes bruv, you waiting for me?" he asked.

Now this was unusual I was expecting some religious brother or at least someone with a beard and dressed like a Sufi but instead this Asian rude boy was beckoning me into the car. This was unusual.

"You know the Shaykh bro?" I asked.

"Yes, bruv, I'm his P.A", he replied laughingly.

I laughed thinking this was interesting and entered the car. The P.A was a young guy, bit of a geezer and as we drove through the streets he simultaneously chatted to me and to friends on his phone. After a while we arrived at the Shaykh's destination and he escorted me into a house to the lounge.

"Shaykh I brought your man", said the P.A

I turned to see the student who I had dismissed earlier and in a split second realised my error.

"Salaam Alaikum, I am the Shaykh".

Did I feel stupid or what? This man was the Shaykh! I shook

his extended hand and sat down on the sofa next to him. As I had noticed earlier the Shaykh appeared of Middle Eastern descent but I learnt later that he was of English descent and had been a Shaykh in the Naqshbandi school of Sufis for many years. He was smartly attired in a pair of trousers and a dress shirt looking every inch the English gentleman.

There was another elderly Asian man who sitting on a chair with his eyes rolled back in his head appeared to be praying. The room itself was small and on the wall was a black shroud with the words "Allah, Rasool, Muhammad". I recognised it as the, "Muhr e Sharif "the seal of Prophethood'. The floor had a black cloth spread over it and there was a circle of sand.

"I don't even know why I am here", I started and then enlightened the Shaykh with my ideas of there are no teachers; there is nothing to get or know, standard non dual communication.

The Shaykh smiled at me and said,

"I suppose that's another way of seeing the same thing".

The result was I was stunned into silence and realised that in that statement he had changed my understanding. I went quiet and then realised I could not sit on the sofa with the Shaykh. Something inside me was telling me to sit on the floor in front of him. I didn't subscribe to the whole idea of people having a strong energy but something about his presence was overwhelming and I was compelled to sit in front of him on the floor. I sought his permission and he replied simply,

"If you like".

I then told the Shaykh my story and he listened intently, at no point did he stop me or ask questions. He just listened. As he listened I looked at him and was aware of the fact that he was looking into the distance. Maybe he was looking at something I couldn't see yet and I felt comforted by this man. Due to my own experiences I knew this man was a man who had gone free. There was a serenity and peace within him and surrounding him that was timeless. He sat in silence and then he spoke.

"I will help you but you must leave Glasgow immediately you are in danger. The one who has done this magic on your friend knows you will try and fight it and as such will attack you. I can though see that he is veiled and it will be hard to find out who he is, but we shall try. Leave Glasgow and I will contact you and tell you what to do next".

I sat there quietly lost in the timelessness exuding from his presence and I wanted to remain there forever.

"Do not worry when it resolves, it will resolve very quickly", he said.

I had been there for hours and yet it felt like minutes.

"It is time for you to go now", said the Shaykh.

As I left the room accompanied by the Shaykh, he looked at me and answered a question I had in my mind but dared not ask.

"Don't worry the magic circle was not for you".

The P.A was outside and drove me to the station, the Shaykh was with us and as we got to the station. He turned to me and said.

"We will meet again".

And with that he was gone; the man I thought was a figment of my imagination had revealed himself to be very real.

I arrived back in Glasgow. I was tired and just wanted to sleep but more importantly I needed to charge my mobile phone. As I put the phone on charge one new voicemail flashed up on screen. I dialled my voicemail and listened.

"Salaam Alaikum brother, this is the Imam. I think it is time you left Glasgow now".

I was stunned, that was exactly what the Shaykh had said to me and now the Imam was saying the same thing to me. I knew that the two had not met and this convinced me there was something behind the message from both teachers to leave Glasgow. I phoned my old friend in Coventry who many referred to jokingly as my other half. He was a good friend of the Shaykh. I explained what had happened and he had one piece of advice for me.

"Get out of there brother, listen I'm going to go one step further and say when people like this speak you don't argue. As a matter of fact just pack, me and next man are going to be there tomorrow morning".

I agreed but part of me was stubborn and thought that maybe I could tough this out. I had been in dangerous situations before, fights, kick offs and generally tense situations but I knew this was an arena I had never fought in before. Tackling black magic was going to be a different affair altogether.

As promised the lads arrived the next day and when I momentarily decided that maybe I could deal with this all hell broke loose and I was literally bundled into a car. In retrospect I had to love them, they drove through the night to help a friend as they were not going to let me stay. They were also both Sufis in the same school as the Shaykh and even if I hadn't taken the instructions seriously I knew they would. Thus I found myself leaving Glasgow for a second time.

The old ways...

I settled back into Coventry and awaited the Shaykh's instructions. I had been told by him that as he was getting old, I would have to do a number of the rituals myself and that he would help from behind the scenes. I became something of a minor celebrity amongst some of the Naqshbandi Sufis in Coventry and received several offers of help and would regularly receive calls for updates as to what was happening.

Although the Shaykh was not the overall head of the school he was held in high esteem by many. Several of the students confessed they would have loved to have been working with him like this. I suppose not being of the school, I was more interested in resolving matters but initially my every moment and Shaykh's every instruction became of great interest to the students.

It was not long before I received my first instruction and I was off to Glasgow again but only for a week. In this week I was to complete a Wazaif four times a day in four different hilly green areas of the city while facing my friend's house. I will not reveal the exact instructions or what I prayed as I feel the Shaykh gave instructions specific to the situation and it would not be wise for anyone to copy them.

The next week became a mad dash as I moved around the

city. I divided my day up by doing the Wazaif between the five obligatory prayers. It was on the first day that I realised the Shaykh's power. While praying my first Wazaif of the day it started to rain and I was alone in the park when out of nowhere a man appeared who to my dying day I will swear looked exactly like the Shaykh if it in fact wasn't the Shaykh. I had heard that a Sufi can be in many different places at once and as the man approached me he smiled and said.

"I think an umbrella would be in order".

Nothing more and away he went. I continued praying and when finished made my way to the Masjid. After a couple of days life settled into prayer and moving around the four points. This took up all day and I would go back to my hotel shattered every night. Exactly seven days later I returned to Coventry.

Again a couple of weeks later I was told to go back to Glasgow and pray. Again I undertook the same ritual. I returned seven days later.

Again a few weeks later I was told to return to Glasgow, again the seven days ritual began but this time with a new twist. I had to collect earth from the four points every day and bring it back with me to Coventry. I undertook this but had a nagging doubt whether any of this was working. I was to be given my answer next time I returned.

I had not kept in touch with the friend I was helping, we had since fallen out. Yet now I noticed every time I went to Glasgow we would meet up coincidentally and her attitude toward me softened. We would talk but when the topic of what had happened between us was brought up she would clam up. I tried to explain but nothing would convince her. Things were going from good to bad and then back again.

I received an email from the Shaykh; the earth I had been told to bring back from Glasgow was now to be kept in a safe place and allowed to settle for seven days. I did this and went about my normal routine.

It was Thursday the day when we did our weekly "Zikr" and I would go along with my friends who were all Sufi aspirants. As I walked into the hall I met the brothers as per usual and my eye settled on one of the brothers, a brother from Africa who was selling little bottles of perfume. He approached me and we exchanged greetings,

"Brother I have here a scent, it is pure Bulgarian rose, the finest in the world" said the brother.

I smelt the beautiful aroma and then I had a thought that I really should purchase a bottle. I decided to buy a bottle and once having purchased it put it in my jacket and forgot all about it. The Zikr as always was lovely and at the end a few of the brothers and I moved onto a fellow student's takeaway where we would all congregate and eat the poor fellow out of house and home. This normally went on till the early hours of the morning and then we would go to the masjid for the morning prayer and then onto home. This night was no different and we pretty much followed the same routine.

A week or so later I received another email from the Shaykh I firstly had to mix in some pure perfume into the earth I had collected and I immediately recalled the brother who had sold me the perfume, what a coincidence I thought, this was freaky but I was glad I had the ingredients I needed.

I also had to divide the earth into five piles and one I had to burn in the house whilst praying and the remaining earth burnt at four different points north, east, south and west from my house. The distance of each point had to be approximately the same as the others. So if the northern point was a mile away I had to make sure the other points were too. I rang one of the Coventry students and asked him to help me. He promptly came to the house and brought with him a map and a torch as the burning had to happen after sunset.

"Salaam Alaikum brother, I've been a student for seventeen years and never have I come across this", he said as he entered the house.

I did not know whether to be pleased by the statement or frightened. Certainly it was an honour to be with the Shaykh and have him help me. I was however tiring of all this and it was becoming a little strange.

We soon found our four places outside the house and set about on our mission. At each point we mixed the earth into the local earth and using old newspaper and lighter fluid to burn the earth into the ground. We received some quizzical looks from a gang of teenagers at one park. The sight of two people burning the earth was a bit strange and after a while they left us alone perhaps thinking we were crazy people. We worked quickly and efficiently from one point to the next and I was glad the student was with me. We made quick work of our task and were done in no time.

"This is as far as I go", said the brother as he dropped me off at the house.

"Jazakallah my brother", I replied as I came out of the car and with that the brother was gone.

I entered my home and immediately went up to the attic where I had prepared to complete the Wazaif. I prayed and meditated. This lasted about twenty minutes or so consisting of prayer with Zikr and a visualisation technique I had been taught. Once finished I sat in silence.

It had been a laborious journey and I had learnt much about myself and about combating the dark arts. I had performed tasks that I was still in disbelief of yet here I was sitting in my attic with a pile of burnt earth. I took the remains and put them back in the jar I was using to store the earth in.

I sat in the lounge alone and felt weak. Since the burning I had dropped in energy, concentration and generally felt really lethargic. The simple act of living was a monumental effort and I struggled to cope with the day to day routine. I was understandably concerned and wrote an email to the Shaykh. He replied promptly and told me it was the effects of the black magic passing over me. At this point I was unconcerned what it was I simply wanted this over and done with.

I was sick and tired of this constant travelling, feeling weak and the constant rituals and prayers. Even the brothers who came to see me remarked on how sickly and gaunt I looked and many were concerned. There in the depths of madness I questioned my very sanity, was this worth it? My goal of going free came up and I realised how far I had diverted from it. I was static, still and going nowhere. I had ground to a complete halt. This was it; it was all over for me.

This sickening state of affairs lasted for weeks and all those around me grew more and more concerned for me. Around this time I received an email from the Shaykh, instructing me to go to Glasgow once more for a week. This time though I was too pray and scatter the burnt earth at four points around my friend's house as well as scatter some across her doorway. I was also to pray while doing this in a clockwise direction. Wearily I agreed and headed off to Glasgow. I was also told that if I felt drained to summon the Shaykh in my heart and ask for energy. I did so on several occasions and felt better for it.

I arrived in Glasgow and immediately started up my prayers and scattered earth across the points I had been told. At the end of the first day I returned to the hotel and went straight to bed. I needed all my energy for the rest of the week so I decided to sleep. I soon drifted off into a deep sleep and then it happened.

Imagine being awake and asleep, fully aware of everything around you but also asleep. This was the strange state I found myself in. I tried to wake and part of me did only to find I was being pinned down. What was pinning me down I did not know it just felt like something heavy and evil. I struggled but to no avail. I was conscious of the fact that I needed to break from these two entities and it was then that I felt something looking at me.

Something intense and dark was looking at me as if I had been held down, so this thing could inspect who I was. The sensation I felt was as if someone had covered me in plastic and was using it to hold me down to the bed. Instinctively as I felt these three entities, one to either side of me and one looking at me, I started to pray. I prayed every verse I could remember. My life depended on it and I continued to pray, for how long I do not know. I just prayed and an arm broke free. I tried to touch the entity looking at me but as I reached out, it dissipated and I found myself slowly breaking free from the hold I was in.

I just lay there. I breathed rapidly struggling to take in as much oxygen as I could. After a while my breathing settled and I struggled to imagine what had happened. I was now in a state which completely freaked me out. I spent the remainder of the night awake neither here nor there. I was desperate to contact the Shaykh at sunrise.

I text the Shaykh at first light and he rang me. I explained what had happened and he listened.

"This is disappointing they are onto us now, you must leave immediately", he said.

I did not protest or say anything; I just took his advice andfled from Glasgow. I was back in Coventry in no time. It had been a strange experience, but now as disappointed as I was my hometown was the safest place for me. I had returned having failed.

The Sufi and the Faqir...

Over the coming weeks I emailed the Shaykh to ask him when I was to go back up again but heard nothing. One day out of the blue I received an email saying it was a good idea for me to go back. That was it, no instructions, nothing. Just a simple message. Go back. The Shaykh had said when we first met that when this resolved it would resolve very quickly and he reiterated this in the email.

I resolved to move up and after saying my farewells to my friends and family I returned to Glasgow. I contacted the single mother and she told me the good news that she was now married and invited me to stay with them until I found somewhere to live.

Once arriving in Glasgow I went straight to her house and met her new husband. The two were very accommodating and the husband had found me a room in a house. I had dinner and then went to my new accommodation. Nothing would prepare me for what I saw.

The house was literally a squat and its occupants were all illegal immigrants. I would be sharing with one of them. The house was a mess and I found it hard to believe that this would be home but hey I needed a place to stay and I was out of options. It was late when I arrived there so I just had time to say hello to everyone and then went off to bed.

I awoke the next day and thought that the last night's events had just been a bad dream but here I was and in the cold light of day it was even worse. I woke up and went to the bathroom and after seeing the state of that and the kitchen I decided to leave as soon as possible. Some of the people had woken up and I introduced myself to the ones I had not spoken to the previous night. They were no doubt as vary of me as I was of them.

They were polite and very accommodating but I could see they were slightly in awe of me. I found them over time to be a genuine group of friends. They were all united in their difficult situation and yet they were ready to share what little they had and to support each other when one or the other was down.

My roommate was a particular case in point when hearing that a friend needed a kidney, he hadn't hesitated to give him his. In the world I came from these people were rare, a throwback to another time when the words honour and respect meant something.

I was constantly shocked when I heard stories of how they were abused by their employers and at times I wished I could stop them suffering like this. Yet this was what they had chosen to do to provide for their families.

As the world globalises and we are increasingly polarised into those who have and those who do not, this situation will rise. The simple act of life will be distorted and we will as a people be a lost generation, not enjoying the simple pleasures of life. Not being able to move forward or even go back. Stuck as my friends were, in our shared drab existence and yet even then in this madness they found time to smile and spend time with each other. I resolved to help these new friends.

There was one man in our house and I marvelled at how he always prayed. Surely I thought god has forsaken you. Why do you choose to pray to someone who has abandoned you and yet this young man would pray and go to work? He did not engage in drinking, drugs or sleeping with prostitutes like some of the other illegals I had met. He kept himself to himself and always when spoken too answered respectfully.

Years later by chance I was invited to a wedding and I went along with friends, not knowing whose wedding it was. My only concern was my friend was singing at the wedding. Imagine my surprise when the groom walked in and it was this young man. In that instant he looked over at me and we smiled at each other. He had finally made it. He had resolved his immigration status and married a lovely girl. I am happy to say he is now a valued member of the community and living a positive life and I recall something he once said to me when we talked.

"Allah listens to all who sincerely call out to him".

Wise words indeed.

This however was the last thing on my mind as at this moment in time, I was stuck in a house of illegal immigrants and the venerable Shaykh had disappeared. In my panic I kept emailing him and one day he replied. The message knocked me sideways. It stated he could no longer help me; however he was confident that everything would be fine. I did not need to hear this instead I needed the Shaykh to tell me what to do and he had decided to disappear. I should have been angry but I remained calm. I suppose I had always known that a man like this would only be around as long as was necessary. I was also becoming less and less concerned about the situation and the more I thought about the situation the stranger it appeared.

I had over the last couple of months climbed up and down hills, prayed, burnt and meditated my way through it all. I had been attacked by otherworld entities and yet none of it had made sense. As I said I was less concerned now about that situation. Maybe the Shaykh had given me all this to do to keep me occupied and to lessen the desire to try and make the situation fit into what I wanted it to be. Maybe instead of black magic he had been instructing me.

I was certainly mentally tougher as a person now and calmer. I was not as quick to anger. Thoughts whirled around in my head as to why I had gone through all this. I failed to understand any of it. It was something I had found when with Sufis. The teachings, the Wazaif everything was designed to reach a certain conclusion and yet everything was subtle.

I recall when I was told to perform certain prayers by the Shaykh that time would stand still. I would drop out of existence until there were moments when I would swear I was not even there and then I would be back in the room. Something had changed and yet I was unsure of it. Was I really fighting black magic or was it something else? Sufis had been known to use deception to teach and yet here I was fundamentally changed but not able to figure out how. The Shaykh was gone and I was nowhere closer to where I needed to be.

Around this time I moved out of the house. I am ashamed to say I packed my bags one day and left without saying a word to my housemates. It was wrong of me and there was no excuse for my behaviour. I ended up living in a village just outside Glasgow with a work colleague and his girlfriend.

For the first time in months I was able to breathe. The village was beautiful and I found myself going for long walks and enjoying the good life. I started to work out and my body took on some sort of shape after the months of constant junk food. I found I was becoming calmer and when friends and Sufis called from my hometown even they remarked that I was calmer. I would talk for hours to them, attempting to verbalise how I felt and what I had gone through.

This was in no way me teaching but an attempt to make sense of the last couple of years. I would go for long walks and just think and think. I became friends with the local villagers and took part in the Gala day. Life was sweet. I was working in a job I enjoyed, working out and finally making some movement towards a decent life. I deserved this, I deserved to be here and you know what; freedom could wait. Life had taken on a beautiful relaxed feeling. It was nice.

Months passed by and my cosy little existence only became better. One of my housemates was suffering from depression and I watched as she finally came off her pills and made a complete recovery. I would often accompany her on long walks and we regularly visited our favoured place locally known as Spectacle e falls. I would wax lyrical about all my spiritual ideas and she would listen and walk with me. One day we reached the waterfall and as it had been raining for a number of days the waters were particularly strong.

I had previously been seen as a bit of a "dodgy geezer" and this change in me as someone spiritually inclined had been observed by my friends with a degree of amusement. I in turn would play up to the role sometimes, pretending to talk in a faux Indian accent to make my point and it was today I would give my finest performance.

As we both stood on the observation deck watching the waterfall cascade down, I spied a bird flying up the waterfall and pointed out to my friend and said in my faux Indian accent.

"Ah yes, you see this bird. You are like this flying, flying against current of life. You must not do this, accept and go with life. Then you will be fine..."

My friend looked at me for a few seconds and then just gave me a huge grin which turned into laughter. I too laughed and we carried on laughing as we left. That one incident characterised to me my time in the village full of much laughter and joy and I felt blessed to be there. It also made me realise, I had started laughing more and was so much more content in myself and the more happier I became, the more life opened itself up to me and the less I concentrated on what was wrong in my life. Life was working now. It was unknown to me, but I was moving towards greater events.

The summer rolled on and I decided to move out of the village. I really liked it here but I wanted to try and resolve this black magic. Although that felt like a minor issue now what was more important due to my constant conversations with my friends about my experiences to go free, meant that the desire was once again rearing its head. I really enjoyed the village but I also yearned to be in the big city. My time there had finished and although I felt sad at that I knew I had to move on. There was a renewed determination to become what I wanted to become. I said my goodbyes and moved on.

Imagine if you will a man from hundreds of years ago. He has no use for technology or worldly goods. He lives on the outskirts of our modern society and has for years single-mindedly and doggedly pursued the goal of going free. Take it further and imagine that he literally exists on a day to day basis and is on no government database or claims any sort of benefits to survive. He simply exists. When he has no food he will go to a gathering and eat there and if he has no home, he will find a park bench somewhere. He lives on a single idea that he will one day go free and all his efforts are directed towards this goal. He has been vilified and denounced for his efforts and yet he goes on.

He seems outwardly mentally unstable and yet when you talk to him you sense that behind the mad exterior lies something so deep and profound that its mere mention could help others attain all they want and yet he does not realise his own greatness. He is to all intents and purposes a failure in life and yet his heart soars and he is free of the shackles that we in respectable society find ourselves bound by. For some time on my journey I was honoured to know this man. He was I felt to all intents and purposes a Faqir.

A Faqir is defined as,

"A wandering dervish who teaches Islam and live on alms".

While my Sufi friend was not strictly a Faqir, (I was to meet a real one later on) he did share many tendencies of a Faqir and as I returned to Glasgow and moved into a flat where he was also staying we struck up a maddening friendship. I say maddening because although we were literally singing off the same hymn sheet at times he could be infuriating and our arguments were the stuff of legend.

Our initial meeting was when he had come up to me as I was stood on a street corner making a phone call and promptly showed me a picture of his Pir or Sufi Master. This had then turned into conversations whenever we met, then debates, then arguments and finally friendship. This friend who was known as "Sufi" by all who met him was a member of the Naqshbandia school a very sober school of Sufis who placed the practice of Sharia above all else.

They claimed their lineage as did all Sufi schools back to the Prophet of Islam Muhammad (PBUH) with one difference from other schools. They were from the lineage of Hazrat Abu Bakr Siddique (R.A), the closest companion of the Prophet (PBUH), other Sufi schools claimed there lineage from Hazrat Ali (R.A.), the son in law of the Prophet. Indeed the school of which I had been a member was known as the Qadriyya and claimed its lineage from Hazrat Ali (R.A). Qadriyya's are known for being very strong Sufis and are not averse to ecstatic behaviour and such things so as you can imagine our conversations were very interesting.

Small differences aside, we got on famously. We were both in a bad situation; living in a cockroach infested flat and in an area dubbed 'the murder capital of Scotland'. Funnily enough when I look back on it I was really happy there. The constant activity and dramas of living in Govanhill or G'hill as we had dubbed it meant that no two days were ever the same.

In an area where all of us were either illegal immigrants, or the socially and generally messed up dregs of society there was a real sense of community. Add into the mix, constant fights, drugs, prostitutes, illegal immigrants and hardened eastern European gangsters you just knew life was never going to be quiet. There were several Masjids in the area too and a couple of Sufi groups trying to help the local populace. As you can imagine I gravitated towards these groups and found myself spending times at different Zikr gatherings and talking to the heads of these groups. I however found that I just couldn't seem to find the answers that I was looking for from these groups and I started again wondering what I was doing here in Glasgow.

Around this time also I finally realised the Shaykh had also disappeared. There was no reply to my emails and I realised I was on my own. This ending however did not really affect me in the way I thought it would. I had become too busy in my day to day existence and quenched the thirst for understanding what had happened. I was for a while content to seek part time and move on with my life. It was having less and less of an impact on my life and frankly I was starting to tire of the Sufi groups all trying to recruit me into their fold. Life would be simpler if I just lived my life.

Maybe there was no grand prize and I had just wasted my time. Maybe it would be an idea to finally face the cold hard fact that I was no more special then the next person. To live a truly brave life, I had to forget this idea of becoming enlightened and just find a job, find a girl, fall in love, marry, have kids, grow old and finally die. Maybe the whole myth of enlightenment had been sold as a sugar pill. That really there was no such a thing but just a way for a person to hide from their own insecurities. Maybe all I had really been doing was lying to myself and as much as I hated to admit that to myself this was the case. I had wasted time and would have been better just toughing it out through life and maybe finding some sort of way of coping with my problems. My knowledge was limited and I was content to leave these painful questions unanswered.

So life settled into a predictable pattern. Work and then home, and then contend with the daily dramas of Govanhill. I was content to live this strange existence because I really did not want to think too much about anything. Sufi was still trying to recruit me into his Sufi school and I was constantly being invited to their meetings. I was happy to go along as there was a free meal at the end of it but mostly because I was starting to strike up friendships with some of the other students.

I did not want to actively seek nor was I actively pursuing the goal of re-joining respectable society. This twilight zone of existence was comforting because I really did not have to think. I did however at this time try to write down what I felt in order to understand what had happened to me but I abandoned writing after reading my thoughts, which were in my mind a garbled mess. I would regularly write and then destroy my writings. I was struggling to understand my experiences and by putting them down on paper just added to the agitation. All this was to change and what I thought to be right would again be questioned.

It had been a particularly trying couple of days at work. I was rundown and just wanted some time to myself. I had decided to take the day off and just stay in bed with the intention of doing nothing in particular. The day was going well until I saw Sufi's name pop up on my phone.

What does he want? I thought. I wasn't happy with this disturbance to my lazy day. I decided to ignore the call. Sufi however had other ideas and had recently acquired a phone and was enjoying his new toy, so kept ringing. After about the third attempt I realised he wasn't going to give the idea up and so I reluctantly answered the call.

"Salaam Alaikum brother where are you, I have a friend I want you to meet".

"I'm in my room" I replied and then the thought hit me. He has brought a Sufi master to meet me. As soon as I had this thought there was a knock on my door and in walked Sufi with an old man.

We exchanged greetings and sat down. My thought had been right there was something about this man. He was most definitely a Sufi and one of the Qadriyya school. I could just tell from his manner and the way he conducted himself. His eyes seemed to dance, a maddening flame flickered in his eyes and I knew he was totally alive. We kept exchanging glances and giving each other knowing smiles.

"I know who you are", I kept thinking.

"I know who you are!"

The man who I will simply call the Faqir started talking, simple ideas and concepts and yet they made total sense. Obviously Sufi wasn't having any of it and kept at the Faqir with his ideas on the Sufi tradition and the importance of following Sharia. The Faqir seemed able to bat all these ideas away with relative ease and something in his easy manner seemed to resonate with me and I felt as I had when I had met the Shaykh only this energy despite being the same displayed itself quite differently.

My earlier suspicions where confirmed when the Faqir

confessed he was of the Qadriyya school, however rather than being a strict Qadriyya Sufi he was from a school called the Qadriyya Noshahi. This was not as uncommon as I used to think. Different Sufi schools do over time combine to create schools that have spiritual teachings from different sources. It ensures that Sufism is always changing, growing and adapting to the times. This has brought it in for criticism from other sects in Islam but Sufis have traditionally just ignored this criticism and carried on with what they do. My mind returned to the conversation which became increasingly simpler and yet more intense. There was such an energy to this Faqir that I felt at points quite ecstatic.

The hours rolled on and yet they felt like minutes and after a while time stood still and there was nothing but beautiful words being heard and spoken. Who was listening and who was speaking no longer mattered? There was simply a beautiful symphony and I felt transported back to another time.

So this is how the old Sufis would have sat around at the dargahs talking, listening and composing poetry. As the afternoon became evening, I realised that I understood this Faqir and everything he said. It all made sense to me and yet his presence was showing me what it was to arrive at the destination. Could it be that this was my true teacher? I tried to fight this idea as I had promised I would take no man as a teacher or give my power over to anyone and yet I felt this urge to take the "Bayat" with this man. As stated earlier the Bayat is the pledge of allegiance the student gives to the teacher and as I sat there I just felt compelled to make this man my teacher.

"Will you take me as a student?"

The words echoed in the room and I couldn't believe I had said them. Time literally stood still and it was as if my very existence had broken under the weight of this statement. The Faqir stared at me. I was desperate for him to say yes. I wanted to be lost in this energy to sit in the company of my Lord to sit in the court of Allah and just stare at his divine countenance. To finally go home, that statement had encapsulated for me my entire suffering and desperation. I wanted to go home, to be free of this suffering and to sit where this Faqir sat. From illusion to reality to finally say

Labaik Allah humma Labaik,

Labaik la sharika laka labbaik

Innal hamda

Wan-ni'mata

Laka walmulk

Laa sharika lak

Translation: *"Here I am at Thy service O Lord, here I am. Here I am at Thy service and Thou hast no partners. Thine alone is All Praise and All Bounty, and Thine alone is The Sovereignty. Thou hast no partners."*

I wanted to pray this, to shout this, to experience this . I wanted this Faqir to show me the way home now. I wanted, I wanted, I wanted.

The Faqir smiled, he knew the fire that burned in me to go free had been stoked. I was on the journey again. After an eternity he answered.

"No, you are not one of mine".

I suppose after this rejection I should have been distraught and yet I wasn't. I was calm and that struck me as very strange. The Faqir talked for a little while longer and then decided to leave. I asked if I could walk him back to where he was staying and he agreed. We walked in silence on a beautiful summers evening. When we arrived at our destination he asked if I would like to accompany him the next day for a walk and I readily agreed. He smiled and with that he was gone.

The next day I awoke early my only desire was to meet the Faqir. Something was different again after last night and as I dressed, I was conscious that I needed to be on time. I was also conscious of the clothes I was wearing. A bright yellow T shirt with the words "Fighting Union" emblazoned across them and jeans with trainers. Surely I thought to myself I could dress more conservatively when meeting such a pious man. I had a chuckle to myself about my attire and then left the house. Little did I know then that the choice of clothes would have a deep impact on my life.

We exchanged greetings and set out upon our walk. It was Friday and a beautiful day. When we reached our bus stop, the Faqir decided he did not want to board the bus just yet and decided to sit on some stone bollards and instead watch the world go by. I decided it was best to keep silent and stood near the Faqir as he sat in silence. After twenty minutes or so, the Faqir stood up and announced we should go now. I followed and within minutes we were on the bus heading into the city centre.

As we arrived we made our way to a small fish market and the Faqir announced that he wanted to buy some fresh fish for later. We purchased the fish and moved on from there. I followed in silence and occasionally the Faqir would ask me to stop and take his picture at some statue or another. I dutifully obliged and found myself acting almost as if I was his student.

I followed in silence, spoke only when I was spoken to and did what was asked of me. It was unusual that he never asked to do any of this, yet it was just happening naturally and not out of some sense of duty. Something about this Faqir just made me want to be with him and respect him and do as he asked. As we walked around Glasgow I answered any questions and was just content to follow him.

Occasionally he would enter teaching mode and tell me about what it meant to teach or to be a Sufi. He would ask me questions and test me to see where I was spiritually. He explained areas of Sufism that I had never been told about such as how Sufis conducted themselves. The subtleties of Sufism, of Sufis he had met and of his teacher. He held his teacher in high esteem and I could see there was much love in his heart for his teacher.

He told me how he had been instructed in the Sufi way and how once he had taken on a job in a pub just to be close to a person who he knew to be his student. It had taken eight months before they had the conversation that he knew they would have and in that time he had done menial work patiently as this was what was meant to happen. I listened to all of this fascinated, privileged to be learning from this man. I was enthralled by his words as he further continued explaining differences in different spiritual approaches and how the Sufi tradition encapsulated other approaches. How Sufis such as Ibn Arabi had come to their conclusions or how others such as Imam Mansur Al Hallaj due to his ecstatic outburst of *"I am truth"* had been summarily executed by the religious orthodoxy of his day.

The day passed like this and I felt with each passing moment I was changing. My very existence was shifting and I was never going to be the same. I remembered what the teacher had said to me when we first met.

"The arrow has left the bow and cannot return"

This in turn reminded me of the famous Sufi saying,

"The moth must fly to the flame, it knows it will burn but it is so captivated by the light that it continues to fly towards the light".

I was definitely burning. As the day came to a close, we ended up back at my flat for a cup of tea and as we talked, I felt compelled to read to the Faqir some of the ideas I had written down so I asked his permission to read. He agreed and as I started reading aloud, he listened in silence. The smile on his face slowly turned into a look of intensity. After I had finished reading we left the flat and we walked in silence back to where he was staying. I was worried as he had not said a word since I had read out my thoughts to him. Finally I plucked up the courage to ask him if I had offended him. I had really enjoyed myself and did not want the day to be ruined by my stupidity.

"I'm sorry, I've offended you, forgive me".

The Faqir looked at me.

"Will I be ok?" I asked, shocked that I had even asked such a question out the blue.

The Faqir continued to look at me and then smiled.

"You're going to be fine".

I felt a sense of relief that I had not offended him. We continued talking and I was happy that he had enjoyed the day and enjoyed my writing. He informed me he was leaving tomorrow and to pop in briefly to see him before he left. I agreed instantly and went on my way.

The next day I went to see the Faqir as promised he was with some people but broke away from them to talk to me. He had some presents for me and I was a bit ashamed that the thought of buying him a thank you present for the time he had spent with me failed to cross my mind.

My present was a CD he had compiled for me with old Sufiana Kalam or devotional songs. He also gave me a bottle of water to drink that he had blessed and gave me a Wazaif to pray that would resolve my problems. I thanked him with a hug. I asked if I could accompany him to the coach station and he replied that we should say our goodbyes now as some other people were travelling with him. I was sad to see him leave and again thanked him for our time together.

"Will I see you again?" I asked

"If Allah wills" he replied and with that the Faqir was gone.

That day will always stay with me forever as a life changing experience, I truly believe I was in the company of a real master and over the coming months that day would make sense to me. Indeed years later little bits of that day are finally understood. Could I say I knew what was happening that day? Not really. Again similar to what I said at the beginning of the book as I change and my thinking and ideas change no doubt I will notice more of that day, understand it better and maybe realize one day why it happened. I am content though to have had such an inspiring day with such a unique individual.

There is however one incident from that day which stands out for me and that was when we met some bagpipe players. The Faqir had decided he wanted to listen to these buskers and as we listened, I noticed a heavily pregnant woman in a pink top and an elderly Asian lady also listening. As the Faqir listened to the music I asked him if there was anything he needed. He replied water and I walked off to a shop to purchase some bottled water. Casually I looked at my watch it was Friday

1.20pm. That moment my life changed.

The following couple of weeks saw me return to my day to day existence, the only difference being that now after meeting the Faqir my seeking had returned with a vengeance. I was spending hours at bookshops and libraries, devouring all I could find on spirituality. Going to see the Sufi groups returned with a vengeance and I engaged in long discussions with them. It became maddening and I phoned the Faqir a few times to try and make head or tail of what was happening to me.

The Faqir was distant as if not wanting to talk to me. In retrospect he did me a service as I really needed to figure this out myself. One day after a particularly rough day I rang him and it degenerated into an argument or more accurately me ranting and raving. I rang back after I had calmed down and apologized and the Faqir replied he loved me like a son. This stunned me into silence and I listened silently to him speaking. At the end of the call I said my goodbyes but little did I know then that this would be the last time we spoke.

I regretted my outburst at the Faqir but at that point I was flying towards the flame, nothing or no one could be allowed to get in my way. My work once again suffered and the maddening desire to go free only intensified. I thought I was slowly starting to lose my grip on reality and I redoubled my efforts to try and live a 'normal' life but no to avail. I once again returned to self-help and started practicing E.F.T (emotional freedom technique) and other alternative therapies. Anything to make the pain of separation disappear I wanted to be whole and complete now and life just was not working anymore. Everything I knew was to no avail now. My experiences, the awakenings, all of it redundant now as I struggled to make sense of it. I felt an urge to phone the speaker. Surely he could help I thought.

The voice on the other side of the line was the speaker's wife, we exchanged greetings and I launched straight into it.

"How can I end this seeking"? I asked.

I knew the answer even before it was answered. Indeed the whole idea of asking a question expecting to receive an adequate answer was futile. I received the answer I already knew.

"You already know, there is nothing you can do" was the answer.

I mumbled something and hung up. My suffering continued. I became increasingly desperate to finally end my seeking and this led to a further deterioration in my work. One day I was called into the office and told my services were no longer required. I knew this was on the cards and yet I reacted badly, calling my boss who had helped me in time of need every name I could conjure up. To his credit he listened silently and offered me his hand. I begrudgingly shook it and left. I was out of work now too.

My personal relationships degenerated at this time too and I found myself angry and argumentative, nothing mattered but being free. It was maddening as I knew everything on an intellectual level and yet it was not enough. I knew something was missing; some piece of the puzzle was just out of my grasp. I suppose I was looking for some Buddha style event to finally realize I was free. So days stretched out and took on a predictable routine. Wake up, dress and attend groups, think deeply about going free and read anything I could find and in this manner my life moved on.

I need to be recognized today...

This simple thought started my day as I dressed for the day. I wore a pair of jeans and a yellow T shirt with the words Fighting Union emblazoned across it with white trainers and left the house. I had to go into the city center to exchange some clothes and I had been invited to a spiritualist church meeting by my E.F.T coach. It was a beautiful day and I was enjoying the warm weather and walk. As usual I was thinking about how to end the seeking and wondered if the meeting could offer a way out for me. I suppose deep down I knew it was unlikely but I harbored the thought it may just do that.

I had come to a point now where looking to end seeking had become a twenty four hour obsession and I was willing to go anywhere and sit with anyone to finally go free. In retrospect it was a dangerous situation I was in as I had long since thrown caution to the wind and was living a totally precarious existence.

I reviewed my life as I walked, many years ago I had decided that to be free would be my solution, in that time I had travelled across the world, moved homes, alienated myself from all that I loved and had experiences that I believed I never could. I had truly changed and learnt much and yet I was now at a point where I was questioning my very reality, my very sanity. How could this have been? Jung talked of the dark night of the soul and I was going through this now. My life was transitioning and I did not know where I was going next. It was maddening, freeing and a hundred other feelings simultaneously. To be obsessed with a single goal was something I had never experienced and yet now every fibre of my being was screaming I need to be free.

It was with this thought that I entered the bookshop and habitually went straight to the religion and spirituality section. Whilst there I spotted Rumi's Masnavi, books one and two. Wow I thought what a find. I had read bits of Rumi and had never thought to read the Masnavi as a whole. I had also for some strange reason kept away from Sufi literature for a while. I suppose due to my experiences with the teacher. To be honest I was disillusioned with Sufism and Islam and that had kept me cynical even when I sat with Sufis or Imams.

However here in front of me was Rumi's Masnavi and I just knew I had to have this book. I hurriedly brought the books and paid for them. I could not believe that I had found these gems. Curiously when I look back I was just drawn to the books and not because I thought Rumi could give me answers but because I needed to have these books. Even though I never bought 'spiritual books' something about these two books told me I had to have them. I left the bookshop with Rumi and happy I had the great Mevlana's books.

I entered the spiritualist church and met my friend. The service soon started and to say I found it comical was an understatement. Do these people not realize that this isn't it I thought, but what was it?

What exactly was it?

What was I sacrificing my life for?

Was it even worth it aiming for something I had no idea about or could it be that on some fundamental level I knew what it was I searched for?

Was it for Allah I searched or was it myself?

What was it?

Infuriating thoughts, can I not just stop thinking?

Just for a moment. Just to be free for a few seconds. Thoughts swirled in my mind and although I knew I had an answer for everything it still was not the answer I was seeking. This was beyond an intellectual knowing and yet how was I to let go of the intellect.

How can I let go of myself?

This maddening feeling.

This desire to be free.

This madness.

This insanity.

This pain.

Can you, my mind not be quiet for a while and let me rest?

The service ended and I walked out of there, none the wiser and a lot more frustrated. I spoke briefly to my E.F.T coach and was invited to a barbeque. I agreed to go and then realized I had to be elsewhere. I moved on and the curious thought once again took life in me.

I needed to be recognized that day.

I was at the railway station buying my ticket to Ayr, the Scottish seaside town where I had arranged to meet a friend and just as I received my ticket my phone rang. I answered. It was my friend; he apologized that he was unable to meet me.

Great, I thought to myself as I had just bought the ticket.

"Ok, no worries", I replied and put down the phone and angrily ripped the ticket I had just paid. Idiot I thought, I was now at a loose end so headed back to the flat.

I was greeted by Sufi as I entered the flat and I just knew we were going to argue and lo and behold we did. This day apart from purchasing the Rumi books was turning into a wash out. The only consolation was that it was a sunny day and after a few more crossed words with Sufi. I was out of the door again. I decided that I needed a nice walk and as I walked through the local park I was taken in by the beauty of the park and the highlands I could see in the distance.

Slowly but surely I calmed down after my argument with Sufi and just sat quietly on the park bench. I had sat on this very bench when I was fighting the black magic and here I was years later. I smiled to myself and after a while I felt calm and happy in myself. Wow a respite from the seeking I thought. I continued to sit there doing nothing in particular. Just watching people go by and just observing. After a while time seemed to have no meaning and I just sat there, thinking of nothing in particular. It was one of those rare moments when I could just sit and stare.

The phone rang and I saw it was my manager from work.

I wondered why he was ringing.

I answered the phone.

"You've forgotten haven't you" he said

"Forgotten what" I said.

"We are meant to be going for a meal you left a voicemail for me", he said.

"Oh yeah I forgot, sorry about that where you at?" I asked.

"I'm at the quay will pick you up, where are you at" he asked.

I told him where I was and we decided to meet halfway. I had totally forgotten about the voicemail I had left on his phone. I had seen his car parked up earlier in the day and left him a voicemail saying we should go for a meal. What with everything going on I had totally forgotten.

This was one of my gripes with this seeking; it was playing havoc with my memory and with me functioning normally. Still it would be good to see my manager as he was not just my manager but over time had become a good friend. He had managed to facilitate my return to work after our boss had let me go. We had lived together in the village and I had learnt a lot from him and over time developed a real respect for this man. He gave his time unsparingly and was always there when I needed to talk.

I had never talked to him about my whole wanting to be free or my mad adventures but I sensed that there was an unspoken understanding on his part as he was from the Asian community and the whole spirituality was never far from the surface. We were people of Temples, Ashrams, Masjids and Baba's, Gurus and Pirs.

Indeed the Indian subcontinent enjoys a rich spiritual heritage and any conversation about spirituality is full of amazing insights from people who have this rich heritage deep in their veins. Sufism, Advaita, Buddhism, Dvaita and other approaches have been instrumental in shaping the Indian subcontinent.

My manager picked me up and we drove to the restaurant. As we got there I reminded him jokingly that he was paying and he laughed in agreement but only if I stood in the queue. I agreed and took his money. Seeing him had really cheered me up and I forgot my bad day and began to find that the day was indeed wonderful. I had book one and two of the Masnavi to read and now I was being dined by a friend.

We arrived at the restaurant and as we walked in I turned to survey the restaurant and I caught sight of a girl looking at me. She was just standing there dressed in a green Pakistani dress. Our gazes met and she smiled a gorgeous smile at me, it was an amazing smile and I was transfixed by her for a few moments. It was just so nice of her to smile and I thought to myself that my day had turned from bad to amazing and now her smile was just like the icing on the cake.

Our gaze broke off and although I wanted to speak to her I knew with it being a Sunday evening the restaurant was particularly busy with Asian families, no doubt she was with family,so I did not want to be disrespectful. I diverted my attention back to the queue.

Having ordered the food, I walked to our table and as I approached there she was again; the girl in the green dress. She was dining with some of her friends and I commenced to approach their table in the mistaken belief that it was my table with the intention of correcting their mistake. My manager however called me over to the table next to them and we settled there waiting for our food. I soon put the girl and her friends out of my mind as we started to discuss the latest shenanigans at work.

Midway through the conversation my manager turned to me and said,

"Geez, I think that girl in the green dress is looking at you".

"Why not, I am a damn fine looking geezer" I replied jokingly.

"No seriously" he said.

"Not my type bro", I replied trying hard to sound casual.

"She's a nice girl", he replied.

"Yeah you're right but not my type", I replied.

I was conscious of the fact that we were packed in a restaurant full of Asians and the Glasgow Asian community was extremely tight knit. There would inevitably be people who knew her, cousins and brothers were always around and I had no desire of fighting today. I was content and satisfied that we had smiled at each other. We soon returned to our conversation but occasionally I would look over to her and her friends. They seemed happy and content and I found myself slightly envious of them. It was a lovely evening, beautiful weather and they were sat at a waterfront restaurant happy. I thought why can't I be that happy?

"Your caesar salad sir".

I turned to see the waiter with our food. As he put the plates down I realized I had not ordered caesar salad. The girl in the green dress looked over at me and smiled,

"Sorry, I think that's my food", she said.

"Oh ok", I replied and asked the waiter to pick up the food and put it on her table.

All of a sudden I had a real desire to talk to this girl. I wanted to know her, to be close to her, to sit with her. So I purposefully started speaking loudly.

As the food was being passed over I smiled and said loudly,

"I'm so hungry I could eat a horse".

This was designed to catch not just her attention but her friends. One of her friends took the bait and asked,

"Are you from Birmingham?"

"No", I replied and the conversation began.

Being salespeople my manager and I soon invited ourselves over to their table and learned a little about them. They had just returned from an Islamic conference and had decided to eat. They seemed like a nice bunch of girls, just living life and having fun. In all of this I noticed that the girl in green dress had sat listening silently.

As per usual the conversation turned to the question of marriage and when I was asked if I was married I explained that I was in a complicated situation. In response one of the girls pointed at her friend and said that her friend a religious sister was looking to marry. Oh great I thought I am being set up with her. I laughed and made some feeble attempt at a joke and then turned to the friend who was obviously the ringleader of this merry bunch and said,

"I'd love to know, is your friend in the green dress single"?

This had the effect of sending the ringleader into excited chatter,

"Yes brother I know her parents, she is a lovely girl. I can talk to them if you like".

At this the girl in the green dress rose and making some excuse about dropping off one of the other girls in the group and the group started to leave.

This was not good I thought of a way of making her stay. I needed her to stay, I was happy and the thought of her leaving filled me with an indescribable sadness. I blurted out,

"Stop! Listen I can tell you your future". It was desperate but she stopped and looked at me intently.

"Give me your hand" I asked and I noticed there was an edge of pleading to my voice and this surprised me.

"I don't give my hand to strangers" she fired back.

"Ok, let me just look at it then please", I asked. This was silly I was desperate for this girl to stay.

She smiled and showed me her palm.

I looked at it and then said something I will never be able to explain.

"You're going to get married and you will really love your husband and he will love you".

She looked at me and laughed and must have found it amusing as she asked jokingly,

"Ok, when"?

"It will be within a year and it will happen" I said boldly, both shocked and bemused at what I was saying, with added flourish I continued,

"I have said this, it will be done".

She smiled her beautiful smile and started walking off, which given the situation was wise. No doubt in her mind I was totally crazy but I asked if I could walk her to her car. She agreed and I walked with her just happy to be by her. Truthfully speaking I just needed to spend as much time with her as I could. I just needed to be around this person. There was something different about her. I couldn't put my finger on it but there was. As we walked I asked,

"So will you marry me"?

She laughed and asked,

"Why, do you have a ring"?

I had a ring my mother had given me from the shrine of Khwaja Garib Nawaz a famous Sufi saint from Ajmer in India and I promptly took it off.

"Yes, do I have to get on my knees?" I asked.

She laughed and carried on walking. I was clearly a source of amusement for her and maybe that was why she was not offended by my behavior. We arrived at the car and she was about to leave with her friends. This was not good and I wracked my brains out for a way to stop her leaving but my mind gave me no clues. We said our goodbyes and as quickly as she had come into my life she left.

Little did I know that I had just met the girl who would be

pivotal in changing my life forever.

Rumi...

After a long week at work I was shattered. Having returned to the flat I shared with my friend Sufi and the illegals as I fondly called them, all I wanted was to be done and finished now. I entered the cockroach infested flat and as usual the blanket of despair just deepened in me. As I went into my room, I caught sight of the two Rumi books I had brought a couple of weeks ago and decided that maybe it would be a nice way to spend the weekend.

Sufi was off to another holy march and gathering somewhere in the north of England and my other two housemates would be working their shifts at their respective restaurants. Now was a good time to start reading the two books. I opened the first book and decided to read everything in the book, even the introduction by the author.

"Why not?" I thought. I have an entire weekend with these two books and I felt compelled to read them in their entirety. The feeling was not dissimilar to the feeling you have when you are so enjoying a book that you do not want to finish it. The only difference was a few pages into the introduction having not even read the Masnavi itself I was feeling like this.

Having read the introduction I turned the page and there it was page one and the famous reed song. It began,

Listen to this reed, how it makes complaint,

telling a tale of separation:

"Ever since I was cut off from my reed-bed,

men and women all have lamented my bewailing.

I want a breast torn asunder by severance,

so that I may fully declare the agony of yearning.

Everyone who is sundered far from his origin

longs to recapture the time when he was united with it.

In every company I have poured forth my lament,

I have consorted alike with the miserable and the happy:

Each became my friend out of his own surmise,

none sought to discover the secrets in my heart.

My secret indeed is not remote from my lament,

but eye and ear lack the light to perceive it.

Body is not veiled from soul, nor soul from body,

yet to no man is leave given to see the soul."

This cry of the reed is fire, it is not wind;

Whoever possesses not this fire, let him be naught!

It is the fire of love that has set the reed aflame;

it is the surge of love that bubbles in the wine.

The reed is the true companion of everyone parted from a friend: its melodies have rent the veils shrouding our hearts. Whoever saw poison and antidote in one the like of the reed? Whoever saw sympathizer and yearner in one the like of the reed?

The reed tells the history of the blood-bespattered way, it tells the stories of Majnun's hopeless passion.

Only the senseless is intimate with the mysteries of this Sense; only the heedful ear can buy what the tongue retails.

Untimely the days have grown in our tribulation; burning sorrows have travelled along with all our days;

Yet if our days have all departed, bid them be gone it matters not; only do Thou abide, O Thou incomparably holy!

Whoever is not a fish is soon satiated with His water; he who lacks his daily bread, for him the day is very long.

None that is inexperienced comprehends the state of the ripe, wherefore my words must be short; and now, farewell!

I closed my eyes and lay back as something overcame me. I went into a trance and lay there just lost in the song. This was incredible and I awoke after a while eager to carry on reading. As I read on I found myself agreeing with everything Rumi spoke of. I found I would read a certain couplet and trance out and just savour what was being said. This was incredible.

I had heard from people who say that whilst reading Rumi, it felt as if their hearts were exploding with joy or that they felt Rumi was talking to them. I now knew how they felt and as I read I continually went into a trance and swooned at the beauty of Rumi's words. I was catapulted back to the time of Rumi and imagined being there as Rumi ecstatically uttered verse after verse and his ever faithful student Hussam al-Din Chalabi wrote down what was said.

I found myself whirling deep down as each word pierced my heart and I knew what was happening was special. There was however one thought that kept coming up continuously. I knew this, I knew all this. The Masnavi was confirming for me what I knew deep down. As Rumi described the journey I found it nothing more than confirmation of what I knew and had experienced.

This had the effect of intensifying what I felt and I continuously went in and out of a trance. Time seemed to cease as I was taken by the Mevlana on a journey and when I came back from this journey I was no longer the same person. The Mevlana had cast his magic and my heart was filled with love. Again there was a shifting in me and as the weekend finished and the reading finished I knew I had moved on. I was closer to my goal again.

Dervish...

I dedicate this chapter which is the most important in this book to the one who burned my soul. Across time we have been brothers and we have fought together. In time we shall meet again and I shall be the one who knows you. I am honored by you and to know you and by our love for each other. There is not a moment you are away from me. I am your Yunus. You are my Shams. Countless times we have met and countless times we have been separated, but in the court of our lord we sit side by side. I will honour your request for anonymity and mention only three incidences from our time together, grant me this as the very least I can do to celebrate and honour you. You are my brother and will always be. Here and in the Akhirah

Wahid.

Brother, he came back from Medina and shaved off his beard.

I reply to this, take me to him for he knows.

Ithnan..

A stranger knocks on a door and a man answers tall and beautiful with fair skin like milk and long flowing hair.

"Jesus" I say.

"Not quite" he replies with a smile

The stranger's heart is taken.

Thalatha...

We sit in silence, he is with me. We are alone. Everyone has left the gathering is over. He looks at me intently. There is wisdom in these eyes that I have never seen before and he says,

"There is no god".

We sit silently and then he speaks again

"This conversation will be talked of for years".

We whirl now

We are close to death

We sense it

We feel it

Faster and faster we whirl

Facing death at every turn

Swords sharpened ready to commit the deed

Kill me, kill me, my only remembrance

As the blade pierces my breast

I breathe my last

The illusion is no more.

I am home now my father.

I have achieved what I wanted.

Death at my father's feet.

Death...

I am sat in my father's old room. I come here when I want to be alone. I come here when I want to be free of my pain. I sit here and think of him and what he meant to me and his impact on my life. Would he have been proud of me, have I become what he wanted me to be. What would he make of me now, my seeking, and my desire to be free?

I am in pain and I want him here to make it all go away. I am tired, I am not sleeping and I have come home for a while to get away from Glasgow and yet I can't get away from myself and these maddening thoughts in my mind. I am unknown to me at the best bit. Sufis talk of the fact that in the end the student is deserted by his teacher, his books and everything. Indeed one of the last veils that can obstruct this seeing, is the veil of knowledge. I am myself obstructing myself. I have been trying to tear down that veil but it's going nowhere.

Who am I?

What am I?

What have I become?

What is this?

What is it to be truly free?

How do I know I am free?

How will I know?

Questions swirl in my mind and I feel tired my eyes heavy from lack of sleep. I'm tired, oh my Lord I am tired. I just want to sleep and yet I know I can't sleep. Not until I figure this out. Not until I go free. My beard has grown and I look unruly. Like a demented mad man. I can hear my family in the next room laughing and joking and I envy them. I just want to be normal but I have no way of knowing what normal is anymore. I am sat here on a sofa where my father's bed used to be. I imagine him there and me sitting at his feet. Him listening to his music and me just sitting there and finally we speak and he tells me how important it is to be educated and live a good simple life.

Past, present and future merge in me and all of this goes on inside me in this moment. Time ceases to be of concern to me and I just sit and stare and think and think and think. Why will this not end?

Like a whirling, something stirs in me. I am thinking and my mind has taken on a thought. I have heard this thought and read this thought. I am this thought. Indeed everyone I have sat with or talked to or read has said this. Slowly this thought starts to take shape, I keep thinking it, hearing it, feeling it, and knowing it. It whirls inside me, rising in me with such a force and power. I keep thinking this thought and thinking. It rises in me, there is nothing now but a thought that refuses to go away. It rises in me, slowly then faster. Whirl away thought, whirl away thought, whirl away. Whirl thought, rise. I need you to rise. I can feel you and as you climb I climb. I am dying, oh my Lord I am dying. Thought, oh thought are you my death? Is my final moment here?

GONE...

Silence Abounds. Everything is still.

I am done. I am finished. I am no longer here. The gravity of this hits me like a punch to my face. I am free. I am that which I have sought. I am free now, liberated and enlightened whatever you wish to call it. I sit there for what feels like an age and I know something has changed and finished. I just sit there. No emotion, no thought, nothing. This is it, this is all there is.

I do not wish to sit in this or do anything at all now. It is all just happening as it is and yet I am here too. I am everything I see and yet apart. Theories, problems everything falls apart in me and there is no suffering. I just sit there. I feel tired now like I have been in many battles, as if I have travelled many years. I am tired I wish to sleep, to sleep and never wake. I don't think I will ever wake now and that's fine now. It is timeless and simple. There is no need for anything, no words, no nothing. It is hard to describe, all I have known is seeking and I am finally seeing and finally I tire even of words or descriptions and I just sit there.

They are sitting with me now my two dear friends, one of them is the brother who took me to my first Sufi gathering, the other a religious brother from the Naqshbandi School whom I have come to know and love. They are in the room with me now fooling around, eating the food they have brought with them and asking me if I am going to join them.

I smile at them and feel an overwhelming love for them. They are friends and I love them so much and I am just happy to sit and stare. I hear sounds sharply, see things in such clarity and just feel love for everything. I have fallen in love with the very life I rejected all those years ago.

I travelled the world, I ran from everything, I loved and lost, hurt those I loved, I blamed the world and raged at it and how it had wronged me. I argued with those who tried to help me and made friends, enemies and enemies, friends. I lied to others and yet the worse and most brutal of lies I told were to myself. Whenever I had a chance to grow to finally become something I ruined it. I pushed away everyone who ever loved me and yet all of that doesn't matter now.

I am sitting here now sights and sounds just happening. Life is just happening in a really simple way. I sit here sometimes watching, sometimes engaging. The need to know is dead and things simply happen now. What I sought was myself and yet I thought it something outside me. The goal of enlightenment is dead in me and I am finally rid of the idea that I am somehow incomplete or not whole. I am life and life is me perfect, complete and whole. A thought arises in this emptiness.

I am tired, I have travelled for years. I need to finally sleep. I have been here for hours just sitting and staring. Taking in the gravity of what has happened.

I leave the sofa that I was sat on and look back. I see my father and I see my life and finally I smile. I am free.

What happened next...

It has been a turbulent couple of years. I have sat with people and communicated my ideas. Some have accepted what I said and some have rejected what I said. I have got out there and am constantly in awe and humbled at the amazing people I meet. I am so much more trusting of life now and after my initial nervousness of speaking I can now speak easily. I have noticed life becomes simpler and even how I communicate has become simpler and simpler and I feel less and less the need to speak now. I find at times all I am doing is providing a mirror for those who come and sit with me. They tend to talk themselves out of the idea of seeking. I remember at the beginning I spoke strictly like someone from the non-dual tradition. Everything was just happening and I viewed life simply in a very black and white way. I found though that although the non-dual communication is very black and white and can be shocking to some, it is no more effective than other approaches.

I had come from a Muslim Sufi background and remembering what happened when I read Rumi I resolved to look at the Sufi form of communication. This had the effect of attracting Sufis into my life and I noticed they used a lot of poetry, metaphor, storytelling, movement and music to put their message across.

This approach had the effect of slowly just seeping into the seekers consciousness and bringing them into a realization they would never have hoped to achieve. I again however found it tended to attract one type of seeker. I resolved to see how I could combine the two.

Both communication methods had their pros and cons and yet combining them and being open to whatever comes up allowed me to speak to people as I felt they would resonate. I found this natural and yet I found it could be taken further and simplified. The initial urge to do this had happened because of an attendee at one of my talks. This lady was a trained singer and had pointed out that although she enjoyed our discussions she wished that there was more poetry and metaphor. I decided to incorporate more storytelling and poetry into talks and found her and others resonating even more with what was being communicated. A one size fits all approach was not going to work and I did not want to be constrained by one approach. A combination of pointers and approaches opened up the arena of communication.

If you look at any religious tradition you will find amongst its teachings the very essence at the heart of everything.

In the Christian Tradition Jesus (peace and blessing upon him) stated

"These things I do, you can also".

In the Islamic Tradition the Prophet Muhammad (peace and blessings upon him) stated

"He who recognizes himself recognizes his lord."

In Buddhism, the Buddha stated

"All that we are is a result of our thoughts. The mind is everything. What we think we become".

Was it not then that the same message was being communicated across traditions and pointed to divinity at the centre of it all, When this divinity spoke to Moses (peace and blessings upon him) through the burning bush, Sufis years later asked the question,

If God can speak to Moses (peace and blessings upon him) through the burning bush can he not talk through man, in reference to the incident and in defense of the statement made by the famous Sufi Imam Mansur Al Hallaj when in ecstasy he declared,

"I am truth".

The Prophet Muhammad (peace and blessings upon him) again stated,

"Allah the Almighty has said: 'Whosoever acts with enmity towards a closer servant of Mine, I will indeed declare war against him. Nothing endears My servant to Me than doing of what I have made obligatory upon him to do and My servant continues to draw nearer to Me with supererogatory prayers so that I shall love him. When I love him, I shall be his hearing with which he shall hear, his sight with which he shall see, his hands with which he shall hold, and his feet with which he shall walk and if he asks (something) of Me, I shall surely give it to him, and if he takes refuge in Me, I shall certainly grant him it".

So I could see that this essence was communicating itself across faiths and across traditions that were commonly known and available, as well as through individuals and places.

Again I thought how else is this being communicated? This led to the musical traditions in world faiths. Muslim Sufis, Hindu Mystics, Sikhs and Gnostics to name a few have used music as a transformational tool. Indeed my experiences of listening to Qawalli (Sufi devotional music) had shown me that different spiritual states could be experienced from listening to music and masters across many traditions had used it as a tool to communicate and teach students. I had seen a modern slant on this and indeed used it myself on occasion to push people through stuck states.

Next then leading from this came movement. Could movement be used to convey this essence? Again the answer was in the affirmative. Whirling was primarily a physical act as was yoga or dance and yet all could once taken to their conclusion lead to a realization of this essence. Rumi the famous mystic once danced the "ruqs" around a tree for three days and nights before becoming realized to this essence. I was noticing that everything in creation was communicating this essence.

This led me to how this essence was described, what it was called in different traditions and ways it was seen in relation to man. I found names such as Beingness, Consciousness, Moksha, Fana, Baqa and a myriad of words which were just revealed to me. There were pointers to this truth, some I was already aware of and some new; Sufism, Non duality, Advaita, Dvaita, Buddhism and the Western Mystery schools I found were all useful signposts for seekers on the road to realization of this truth.

Some pointers such as the Non dual tradition said there was no path or even anything to obtain. Some such as the Sufi, Buddhist and Dvaita traditions laid out a clear path that could be used to reach a liberated state. I found each contradicted the other and yet all made sense in the bigger picture and after a while the seeker could see that the contradictions just disappeared. Where did one start and the other finish? I was reminded of a passage I had read in the Bhagavad Gita,

"A wise man knows when to go forward and when to stop".

This verse I found pointed to a wisdom and a trusting that gave me great freedom in my communication. At the beginning of my talks I had noticed that I did not sound totally non dual in my communication and I was quoting Rumi and other Sufis. As I carried on however I realized that there was no standard way of communicating to a group of people or even an individual.

This was most definitely a case of one size does not fit all. Again the communication changed and I found it simple, elegant and more resonant. Also due also to the fact that I had such a torrid time when I was with the teacher and because I was unable to attend talks or buy books when I was seeking, I had developed my own way of communication.

You are reading it now. In the Sufi tradition it is known as scattering where disparate parts come together to form a whole teaching. I chat as I say to people whom I meet and yes it may not make total sense if one section is taken out and interpreted, however once the whole thing is heard or listened to it makes total sense. A symphony is at play here.

Am I aware of this when it is happening, yes and no? I remember once reading an interview with a Non dual teacher and he stated that sometimes it is almost as if he is watching what is being said and at other times there is absolutely no separation between words and the speaker. It is a case of words form and questions are answered. There is a trusting in this.

I am not learned in any theological tradition and yet I find I just say things which make sense. I once decided to listen to an interview I had done with an American website. Now this is not something I am in the habit of doing as once the interview is done I generally just move on. I decided however to listen to it and was amazed that questions where just answered and everything just flowed. Is this channeling? I would answer no it isn't. It is something different, a trusting, a knowing, a simplicity. It just works and that is all that matters.

As I went further I noticed I started to move away from my non dual position, not abandon it, I just moved on from it. I suppose the initial movement from it was when I had met the Shaykh and his answer to my statements had shaken me. As I delved further I started to see that there was something that could be done to try to become liberated. I had experienced being out of myself and not there when I had done Zikr and the Ruqs.

Further to this I had read that Nisargadatta Maharaj a famous Indian sage had attained enlightenment by repeatedly repeating and meditating on the words "I AM I AM". This was something that had been prescribed to him by his Guru. After two years of repeating this mantra he had gone free and yet on the other hand there were just as many people who had spontaneously gone free. Instead of rejecting one view and moving away from it, I decided to keep it and add this new perspective.

I was unknown to myself integrating my experience and expanding my understanding of this truth. This was liberating as after the initial experience I had struggled with the belief that I could be free. What I mean by this is that I knew I was free but unable to believe that it could happen to someone like me. After all when compared to the saint and sages of old, who had prayed and meditated and had moved from their homes and travelled to distant lands where they remained for years. I had been released from the burden of seeking relatively lightly.

This was resolved when the thought formed in my head that why couldn't I or anyone for that matter go free. Was this not open to all? Was it really the preserve of holy men or was it not a possibility open to all. Further to this reading of Sufi Literature and remembering the stories I had been told during my time with the teacher reminded me of the countless thieves and robbers who having met with Sufis or sincerely repented and come to this truth. I concluded that grace was open to all and it heartened me knowing that it was available to all, from saint to sinner. So here was another string to my bow. I also found sincerity and earnestness was another way to approach this truth.

I also noticed how synchronicities and other such abilities made themselves available to you. Not in the sense that they were turned on at will, although no doubt if the development of these abilities was developed it could be, but in the sense that sometimes I would go to places, meet people or be in a situation which was then useful for something else. A classic example is from my first talks in Glasgow.

I had decided to go to the library. I had a few hours to kill and thought I would go and have a read. Whilst there, I happened to chance upon a book on Synchronicity. The book was well written and having time I decided to read it as I had a few hours spare. After I had finished the book I left as it was time for the talk and as the talk started one of the first questions was,

"Could you tell us about synchronicity?"

I smiled as the realization dawned upon me that nothing is ever wasted. Every bit of your life serves some purpose; whether it is reading a book, that failed relationship, your relationship with your family, depression or having a weight problem. Everything is teaching and showing you something and what it shows you will always serve you. Life really is that simple and efficient.

Sometimes if you examine your past, you find clues as to what your future holds. Hence some psychics actually derive the future from your past. What you also find is when this truth, which you already are, makes itself known to you, a real sense of empathy develops with the other party and it may appear as if you know them. Hence you will hear statements such as

"Oh my god I was just thinking that!"

"You're reading my mind!"

This is because going back to the Non Dual tradition, there really is no other and in itself you are only ever having a conversation with yourself; however I felt this again was just one part of the picture. What would show me the other side?

Dvaita Vedanta offered the answers and complimented what I

knew of the Advaita/Nondual tradition. This was the sister philosophy of Advaita (from which the non-dual tradition had stemmed). The other side of the coin. As I read one argument it increased my understanding significantly.

Dvaita scholars have been involved in vigorous debates against other schools of thought, especially Advaita. Whereas Advaita preaches that Atman (Soul) and Brahman (God) are one and the same, which is not evident to the Atman till it comes out of a so-called illusion. Madhvacharya a follower of the Dvaita tradition put forth that Brahman (God) and Atman (Soul) are eternally different, with God always the Superior one stating.

"If you feel there is no God, how do you explain as to why you cannot free yourself from the limitations on Earth? If you feel YOU are the one in control of everything (as Advaita preaches that Soul and God are one and the same) then why can you not enjoy eternal happiness and remain subject to sorrow and pain (as God is supposed to be an eternity of happiness)"?

As my understanding continued to evolve, I questioned everything I had ever known and noticed my understanding of this was getting simpler and simpler. Things just made sense and I had no idea how and why. I constantly put aside ideas and concepts that failed to serve me. This had a disconcerting effect on those around me and yet to me there was only really one constant and that was change.

Bodies change, worlds change and everything changes, so why not the understanding of truth. Yes it is eternal, whole and complete but viewing it through one lens just does not do it justice. Is it not better to keep it open and see it from as many different viewpoints as possible? No doubt you will settle at some point depending upon your viewpoint. We are all unique and to celebrate this uniqueness and diversity it creates in understanding of truth can only be beneficial for those looking to lift the veil of seeking.

At this time I was asked whether I was still seeking as my viewpoints were changing rapidly. The only way I can best describe it was I had moved from seeking to seeing. There is a subtle difference because I was not looking for an answer but instead as the Sufis would put it I was beholding the glory that was me. I was exploring my very essence my very being.

I moved on and found myself increasingly speaking less and less in talks, content to let others talk and just facilitate what was going on. Silence seemed to be the watchword of the day and I felt that words would never be adequate to describe this. Yes there had been some incredibly insightful books written about this and yet all were pointers. Maybe by exploring pointers further I would be able to communicate even more effectively. This reminded me of the Sufi teaching tale of the men with the grape, which was narrated by Idries Shah in his book, The Sufis.

"A Persian, a Turk, an Arab, and a Greek, were arguing as to how they should spend the single coin they possessed. The Persian suggested buying angur, *the Turk wanted* uzum, *and the Arab wanted* inab, *while the Greek suggested buying* stafil. *Another traveller, who was a linguist, asked them to give him the coin and promised to satisfy the desires of all of them. When he was given the coin, he brought grapes for them. On seeing this the Persian recognised them to be his* angur, *the Turk his* uzum, *the Arab his* inab *and the Greek said that in his language they were called* stafil. *The travellers are the ordinary people of the world. The linguist is the Sufi. People know that they want something because there is an inner need existing in them. They may give it different names but it is the same thing."*

I had seen the cover of the Idries Shah book "the Sufis" and was struck by the image on the cover. It was a face made up of individual faces. I remember looking at it and speaking to the Dervish and saying yes I understood why it was so. Now I decided to explore further.

Very little is known of the Sufis or their schools or even their teachings. If you ask two different Sufis about Sufism it is likely that you will receive to get two disparate explanations and yet there is a unity and clarity amongst them about their teachings. Indeed one of the most famous Sufi sayings is,

"Peace with all, enmity with none."

To me this indicated that Sufis do not really have conflict in amongst themselves or with other approaches. If this was the case then Sufis really did have a most clear and complete teaching. I noticed that whenever any famous Sufis had passed away their funeral was characterised by many people of different faiths attending. This was further echoed in their teachings. The Masnavi of Rumi encompasses all faiths even though it was written by a Muslim mystic. Everyone I have ever talked to has told me regardless of their respective faith how it has touched them. Indeed the writings of Rumi and his practices have been adopted by people across the Middle East and across the world.

It was the Reed song that inspired the whirling which as it travelled across the silk road with Sufis such as Khwaja Garib Nawaz, Shah Nizamuddin Awliya and Amir Khusro became Qawalli which was a music form that helped many to Islam in Hindustan, now known as modern day India. This led me to see that Sufis were very adaptive in how they taught.

Another Sufi known as Prince Dara Shikoh when encountering Advaitic thought did an extensive study to concluding it was similar to Sufi thought and this led to Sufi thought becoming mainstream in India. Indeed something similar to Advaitic thought was put forward hundreds of years earlier and credited to the Great Andalusian Sufi Ibn Arabi.

The theory of Wahdut ul Wajood could be seen to be similar to Advaita. Wahdat ul Wajood literally means unity of existence and upon reading about it; it struck me as similar to Advaita. The theory has been seen as somewhat controversial and later Sufis countered its central premise with Wahdat ul Shahud or Unity of Witness, this argues that God and creation are totally separate. Further evolution of these theories led to many saying that what was being discussed was just differences in language.

I was seeing that unlike Advaita and Dvaita which were in essence two separate teachings, a fuller picture could be found in Sufism as both viewpoints of looking at reality where encapsulated in the one teaching but again the Sufis were similar to other approaches in the sense that language could illuminate but also hinder understanding. I often found that two people could be saying the same thing yet disagree. Language was then constricting and yet liberating.

The picture of the face within the face and the story of the grapes offered much in seeing different aspects of the same reality. I found that as the idea of seeking was let go of and resting occurred communication and even silence became clearer. The idea of peace with all and enmity with none further resonated with me.

"This too shall pass" is another saying of the Sufis and I found that following it made things even simpler. Knowing that good or bad events would pass led to equanimity in emotions and after a while good or bad emotions seemed to lose their charge. The natural conclusion of, "this too shall pass" reminded me of a verse in the Masnavi,

"Out beyond ideas of wrongdoing and right doing,

There is a field. I'll meet you there.

When the soul lies down in that grass,

The world is too full to talk about.

Ideas, language, even the phrase "each other" doesn't make any sense.

I shall meet you there"

Eager to see other colours in the rainbow I looked at psychology and the self-help movement and again found that this was to be discovered there also. The American author Robert Anton Wilson in his book Prometheus Rising talked of spiritual experiences as advanced brain changes this was inspired by Dr Timothy Leary's Eight Circuits of Consciousness, which had in turn been inspired by the Sufi Enneagram and Patanjalis sutras of yoga. These were ideas I had previously practised when with the Sufis. Indeed certain Yoga and Sufi breathing practices can be seen as very similar.

Onward I looked and I could see that this knowledge was in me and outside of me and was always communicating itself. I was reminded of the Quranic verse

"Verily there are signs for men of understanding."

I had always felt being a Muslim in the west left you at a disadvantage and now as I delved deeper into Islam I realised that was in itself a complete teaching. The Sufis had stated;

"Granted the world is an illusion, we still have to live in it"

And I realised by following both the internal aspects of Islam i.e. Sufism and the external aspects i.e. the Sharia (Islamic law) a person could attain a real balance that affected every aspect of their lives, from health, wealth, relationships, spiritual progress and ultimately enlightenment.

The inner reality; the Batin, and the outer reality, the Zahir were balanced.

I read how Sufism encompassed seeking with or without a physical teacher, in a school and out of it too. Indeed all approaches are found within it from Wadhut ul Wajood to Wadhut ul Shahud. Both sides are represented as there are two sides to a coin.

The linguistic challenges I had faced in communicating it were calmed and I realised that however I communicated it; it was still in tune with essence.

Apparent contradictions of destiny and free-will were seen through and there was an accepting and yet a dynamism of being able to change things too. I was reminded of a line from a poem written by Sir Allama Iqbal.

"In the glance of the friend of Allah (swt) I have seen the destiny of millions change."

This brought up the question of transmission, could this knowledge be transmitted, if so how? Yes there was the argument of how could it be transmitted when it was all one? Yet there were stories of Sufis who transmitted this knowing.

The Great Sufi Bayazid Bistami narrated the story of how he was woken up. On the road to Makkah on his way to perform the Hajj pilgrimage he came across an old man, who asked him,

"Where are you going Bayazid?"

Bayazid replied he was going to Makkah to perform the pilgrimage, the Hajj.

The old man smiled and said to Bayazid,

"Circle around me seven times and your hajj will be done".

Bayazid promptly did this and as he was circling around the old man, he realised his heart was being pierced with some sort of energy that was emanating from the old man and this promptly woke him up. Liberation from the dream had occurred.

Other such stories made themselves available to me for example the story of a Sufi who had attained such a level of spiritual power that he veiled his face. This was because a single glance would render the viewer of his face totally realised. Again I digested it all and as it added to my worldview I realised this was so much more than I had ever realised.

Life was characterised by constantly realising more of this divinity. As I read further of the Sufis and how they had come into being. Questions on ego, the role of the teacher and waking up without a physical teacher, the correct respect when meeting the teacher and the use of poetry and music to affect a state were all answered and yet with all of this knowledge there was so much more to it.

Just of the written word the Quran states,

"If all the trees on the earth were pens, and all the sea (were ink), with seven more seas added thereto, the words of God (His decrees, the acts of all His Names and Attributes manifested as His commandments, and the events and creatures He creates) would not be exhausted in the writing. Surely God is the All-Glorious with irresistible might (Whom none can frustrate, and whom nothing can tire) the All-Wise".

Yet that which was in the "batin" (that which is hidden) was even more. There was a resonance with this way and how simple principals could be used to come to realisation, for example consider this; Sufis believe that our life and death are written as is our sustenance, who you will be with and the children you will or will not have and all of this appears as and how is needed .

The only choice then needed is whether to live life lawfully or unlawfully. This leads to a sense of relief that most of life's big problems are dealt with and yet we see around the world, people trying to earn more, eat more and enter into negative relationships even though by being patient and trusting everything would appear as and when it was needed.

Living using these Sufi principles leads to what the psychologist Mihaly Csikszentmihalyi describes as flow states. There is a sense of ease to everything however should you fall out of this flow state then you can use another Sufi maxim to make sure there is balance in your life. The maxim of this too shall pass was talked of earlier was and can be used by anyone to come to the realisation that all things are temporal and will pass and lead to what is beyond the temporal and is real.

Simple Sufi truths can lead the seeker to truth. Some of these you have now read and some you will see for yourself for as Allah (swt) states in the Quran,

"When a servant takes one step to me I take ten towards him".

This shows that when you seek, something seeks you too

You may have noticed that this aspect of Sufi thought I highlight depicts something beyond you and yet most seekers are led to believe it is in them. This is also correct, the reason I highlight this is because it is equally valid, do not discount one approach in favour of the other as you limit yourself. It also supports the Dvaitic argument I mentioned earlier and those who follow Wahdut ul Shuhud. Also by putting the destination and goal outside of you leads to less pressure upon the seeker and humility. To say it is beyond my control may lead to a letting go of and a sense of ease as the popular saying states,

"Let go and let God".

The Sufis of old knew and practiced this. In gatherings where states of ecstasy were attained whether by dancing, music or poetry the Sufi would point outside of themselves and say Allah Allah Allah. As this practice moved through the ages in certain cultures it was adapted and used to convey something similar. In the Spanish culture the word Ole Ole Ole finds itself derived from the time when Sufis or artists said Allah Allah Allah. Could this be seen as channeling or the spirit works through me?

So in realizing your true nature how do these differing schools of thought assist? Where does one approach help and where does the other? Each approach has its own particular way of seeing things and on a moment by moment basis can be used to recognize the very freedom that is sought. It is all dependent on the seeker, their story and conditioning.

Consider a walk in the country in viewing that which is outside us. We can see that it offers clues as to the true nature of existence. The sun rises and sets. Oceans rise and fall and life follows a certain ebb and flow. This familiarity is a natural law and shows us there is order. We are part of this order not separate. We are part of the whole. It is us, the apparent duality points to the whole and yet the seeker looks to reject the dream believing there is something better and wishes to outright reject this duality even though it moment by moment offers us an invitation to awaken to our true self.

The miracle once this order is seen is happening right here and right now. An order which allows us to be, to explore what we really are. This order allows us to function for how disconcerting would it be if what we take for granted ceased to exist and we no longer were provided with an opportunity for recognition of what we are within the dream.

Taken further one wonders who has put this order in place. It is here that we enter into the realms of what is this entity and what it is called that ensures this order. There are various names, Allah, Brahman and God. It is really your choice. Go beyond the name and look at this essence how it is ordering all events including your day to day existence. It is making itself known through its creation. The Quran states at this point,

"I was a hidden treasure I wished to be known".

The question that could be posed is to whom?

If we carry on this line of thought then we can see to that which reflects its existence because according to the ideas of Dvaita and Wahdut ul Shahud, we are a reflection and a witness. So that which is real is being known to its creation, its witness. The Sufi idea of the divine spark comes into play here that we contain a portion of God, or our soul is partially created in the image of God and hence the hidden treasure is known to itself by itself. This idea of the divine spark alsobalances the two approaches of Wahdut ul Wajud and Wahdut ul Shahud. The balancing is that which is in the centre of the two approaches, the seeker looking to recognize internally or externally their true self.

As the Sufis state

"A man went looking for Allah and found himself

Another man went looking for himself and found Allah"

This realization that either through God's signs and by pursuing practices laid down by those who came before or even by the simple task of observation and self enquiry that realization can lead to annihilation and taken further a state of permanence in Allah, fana (annihilation) and baqa (permanence with Allah). The drop of water is reunited with the ocean and as such loses all sense of self only to return as self.

Hence now the seeker can realize all of creation is part of him. In the word of Sufi Bayazid Bistami;

"Glory be to me! How great is my majesty!"

In seeing everything as part of him and dropping out of the illusion what is experienced is the real but with no desire to claim the experience. In its simplest form life or the idea of a life is just happening. No more or less significant as anything else. Indeed everything is emanating and returning to the same source. With source being the only significant entity, it is recognizing itself and seeking itself and finding itself simultaneously. Everything appears. All manner of opposites are actually one and the same. The example of a rainbow would be apt as whilst it encompasses an array of colours it is in fact one whole. It can be seen as in the micro for example the individual navigating a world which appears as separate or in the macro as the entire entity observing itself.

This begs the question, what then speaks when the illusion is seen through? Divinity abounds in the very essence of what is. Death is vanquished; the idea of an ebb and flow of life is made redundant. Ideas of being in the moment or in time are equally redundant and nothing remains but the essence. All ideas then of some temporal reality dissolve away and all there is THIS.

In these two approaches coming together all that is seen is IS. It watches itself and is itself. It knows when to go forward and when to stop. It sees the total picture and yet is the picture. It is the fool and the wise man too and it is in every approach and yet outside it. It is both a Scholar and a Sufi. It cannot be encapsulated in words and yet it's words show us truth. It is here and now and yet a destination to be travelled to. It is ecstatic and humbling.

It loves and yet is a ruthless task master. It moves you and yet silences you. Its reliance brings untold treasures and yet it gives us the ability to create. It has clearly shown us the way and yet many will still not understand the simple message conveyed as it chooses to blind them to the light.

It offers salvation to as many as it damns. It grants life and death and yet both are a game it plays. It is maddening and yet the sweetest sanity. Institutions, religions and holy men have all claimed it as their own and claim themselves as its custodians. Some claim they know it and some say they do not and yet we sense it resides in our heart and is all around us. Intuitively it is grasped at and yet even intuition is not enough and fails. It is and it is the only real constant. Even masters have asked.

What is it?

What is it?

What is it?

It is over awing.

It is the lifting of veils between the lover and beloved.

The ending of separation and yearning.

It is an expanse that is liberating when seen.

Earth shattering to the psyche and yet it is the only way to live.

It is your birthright.

It is you.

Did you think I'd forgotten...

I am walking down the street and going nowhere in particular. It is a nice day and I have decided to go for a walk. I am lost in my thoughts and what thoughts they have been! Life is simpler now and I am finally happy. I am wearing a pair of blue jeans and a yellow T shirt with the words Fighting Union emblazoned across it. It is a beautiful day and I am blessed to be here. There is a bounce in my step and a smile dances upon my lips. A car stops ahead I smile as I recognize this car and for me this completes a chapter I have been waiting to complete. I walk towards it and look in,

"Hello" she says

"Hello" I reply and look at her and smile.

We are talking now. Words are forming and an effortless symphony is at play here. She shows me a clip of music being played. Some bagpipe players are playing their tune and as I watch a grainy video, I see a man walk past. Yellow T shirt, blue jeans.

"It was Friday 1.20pm when that video was shot", I say

She checks and confirms I am right.

"How did you know?" she asks.

I smile content to remain silent and take in all I see.

This is where my journey completes and yet this is where my journey begins. This is the paradox of my life and the reason behind my writing this book.

The End...

Glossary

Advaita Vedanta: A Vedantic doctrine that identifies the individual self (atman) with the ground of reality (Brahman). It is associated especially with the Indian philosopher Shankara (circa 788–820).

Akhirah: an Islamic term referring to the afterlife. It is repeatedly referenced in chapters of the Qur`an concerning Yaum al Qiyamah, the Islamic Day of Judgment, an important part of Islamic eschatology.

Allah: The name for God, the Supreme Being, in the Arabic language; the common name for God in Islam.

Atman: The spiritual life principle of the universe, especially when regarded as immanent in the individual's real being. A person's soul.

Batin: The interior, the esoteric; as al-Batin. "the interior, " it is one of the ninety nine Names of Allah, the opposite of Zahir

Bayat: An oath of allegiance to the spiritual master.

Baqa: Subsistence, permanence; the state of one who has been reintegrated in the spirit and has intuitive knowledge of the absolute; the opposite of fana

Brahman: The single absolute pervading the universe and found in the individual (Atman).

Buddhism: Asian religion/philosophy founded by Siddartha Gautama in North East India in the fifth century BC.

Dargah: The tomb or shrine of a Muslim saint.

Dervish: Member of muslim order (sufi) who has take a vow of poverty and austerity. First appeared in 12th Century and known for wild or ecstatic ritual namely dancing, whirling or howling according to practice of order they belong too.

Dvaita Vedanta: Sanskrit word meaning Duality. Name of sub school in Vedanta tradition of Hindu Philosophy. Founded by 13th Century scholar Madhvacharya

EFT: Emotional Freedom Techniques, or EFT (often known as Tapping or EFT Tapping), is a universal healing tool that can provide impressive results for physical, emotional, and performance issues. EFT operates on the premise that no matter what part of your life needs improvement, there are unresolved emotional issues in the way.

Eight Circuits of Consciousness: Theory proposed by Dr Timothy Leary. Concerned with Eight Circuits or gears each working with its own layer of reality. It finds its origins in Patanjali's sutras of yoga and the Sufi Enneagram.

Enneagram: From the Greek word Ennea meaning nine, The Enneagram is a nine-sided figure used in a particular system of analysis to represent the spectrum of possible personality types.

Fana: Extinction, evanescence; the extinction of all that blocks the individual from union with Allah; the opposite of Baqa

Faqir: (plural Fuqara): poor man; a seeker who has the quality of poverty in a spiritual sense (faqr); an adherent to the Sufi Path, an initiate.

Gaddi Nashin: The spiritual successor a descendant of a Sufi or Pir and in some instances descendant of a disciple of a Sufi, A Gaddi Nashin particularly tends to the shrine which is made over the Sufi's tomb, known as a Mazar. The Gaddi Nashin is a key person who held and leads the traditional Sufi rituals in Dargah's daily activities and particularly during Urs (death anniversary)

Hadith: Sayings of the prophet Muhammad (Peace be upon Him) with accounts of his daily practice (the Sunna), constitute the major source of guidance for Muslims apart from the Quran.

Hazrat: An Honorific title used to honour a person. The literal translation is the presence.

Imam: The person who leads prayers in a Masjid.

Islam: A monotheistic faith as revealed by Muhammad (peace and blessings upon him) the prophet of Islam.

Ithnan: Arabic term for number two

Jazakallah: Arabic term meaning "May Allah reward you (with) goodness"

Karma: The sum of a person's actions in this and previous lives that decide their fate in future existence.

Khilafah: An Arabic name or title which means "successor" or "steward". It most commonly refers to the leader of a Caliphate, but is also used as a title among various Islamic religious groups and orders.

Mantra: A word or sound used to aid concentration in meditation.

Muhr e Sharif: The physical seal (signet ring) worn by the Prophet Muhammad (Peace be upon him) and used by the Prophet (Peace be upon him) on several letters sent to foreign dignitaries.

Masjid: Muslim place of worship

Masnavi: Spiritual classic composed by Maulana Jalaluddin Rumi composed of six volumes.

Maulana: Meaning our master can also use Mevlana

Mazar: A Muslim shrine or enshrined tomb

Mevlana: Turkish term meaning our master can also use Maulana

Naqshbandia: One of the four major schools of Sufism. It traces its lineage back to the prophet Muhammad (peace and blessings upon him) via his friend and first Khalif of Islam Abu Bakr. The only school of Sufis to do so.

Non Duality: Meaning not two or one undivided without a second

Patanjali Sutras of Yoga: Influential work on Yoga philosophy and practice written by the Indian sage Patanjali

PBUH: These letters are abbreviations for the words Peace Be Upon Him

Pir: The term used in the Indian subcontinent to address Sufi masters

Qadriyya/Qadri: One of the four major schools of tasawwuf named after the great Shaykh Abdul QadirJilani

Qadri/Noshahi: School of Sufis combining both the Qadri and Noshahi methods of Sufism

Quran: Holy Book of the Muslims

Qawalli: Muslim Devotional music associated with the Sufis

RA: Radhiallahu 'Anhu meaning may Allah be pleased with

him/her, this is an expression to be used by Muslims whenever a name of a companion of the Prophet Muhammad (PBUH) is mentioned or used in writing.

Rizq: All aspects of a person's subsistence and livelihood fall under the definition of *rizq*, including but not restricted to wealth, status, business and children.

Ruqs: A Sufi practice of whirling, dancing and ecstatic movement, usually done when listening to Qawalli

Salaam Alaikum: Islamic Greeting meaning Peace be unto you

Shaykh: Spiritual master or guide in the Sufi Path who has permission or authority to teach others the way of realisation.

Sharia: The religious law governing the members of the Islamic faith. It is derived from the religious precepts of Islam, particularly the Quran and the Hadith

Subhanahuwata'ala: Meaning the most glorified, the most high

Sufi: A Muslim ascetic and mystic on the Sufi Path of self-realisation (Tasawwuf)

SWT: When writing the name of God (Allah), Muslims often follow it with the abbreviation "SWT." These letters stand for the Arabic words "SubhanahuWaTa'ala," or "Glory to Him, the Exalted." Muslims use these or similar words to glorify God when mentioning His name.

Tasawwuf: Islamic system of mysticism also known as Sufism

Thalatha: Arabic term for number three

Wahid: Arabic term for number one

Wahdut ul Shahud: "apparentism" or "unity of witness" holds that God and his creation are entirely separate. The opposite view of Wahdut ul Wajood

Wahdut ul Wajood: Unity of existence, Unity of Being, an idea popularised but falsely attributed to Ibn Arabi the great Andalusian Sufi

Walaikum Salaam: Arabic greeting meaning peace be unto you too. Used in reply to Salaam Alaikum (peace be unto you)

Wazaif: Literally meaning Amount. Recitals of various prophets mentioned in Quran in times of difficulty. Such recitals are beneficial in removing hardships or afflictions when undertaken

Yoga: Spiritual and ascetic discipline, a part of which, including breath control, simple meditation, and the adoption of specific bodily postures, is widely practised for health and relaxation.

Zahir: The exterior, the exoteric; as az-Zahir. "The exterior," it is one of the ninety nine Names of Allah; the opposite of Batin

Zikr: Remembering, remembrance of Allah; the invocation of one of the Names of Allah

Printed in Great Britain
by Amazon